The HUSBANDS' Book

The HUSBANDS' Book

FOR THE HUSBAND WHO'S

Best AT Everything

JIM MALONEY

Michael O'Mara Books Limited

First published in Great Britain in 2008 by
Michael O'Mara Books Limited
9 Lion Yard
Tremadoc Road
London SW4 7NQ

A CIP catalogue record for this book is available from
the British Library.

Papers used by Michael O'Mara Books Limited are natural,
recyclable products made from wood grown in sustainable forests.
The manufacturing processes conform to the environmental
regulations of the country of origin.

ISBN: 978-1-84317-326-7

3 5 7 9 10 8 6 4 2

www.mombooks.com

Typeset and designed by Ana Bjezancevic

Printed and bound in Great Britain by Clays Ltd, St Ives plc

To Alison, the perfect wife.

Contents

CONTENTS

Introduction

First, the good news: being married is officially good for a man. According to research done by some clever chaps in various laboratories, it's been found that married men live longer and more fulfilled lives than men who never tie the knot and cry themselves to sleep every night. (That last bit's just a hunch and not backed up by any scientific studies, but it's probably not too far wide of the mark.) So, that's the good news.

However, there's bad news too. Well, not bad news exactly, just something you need to be prepared for: married life can be hard. Bloody hard sometimes. A good marriage is like a fine cheese or wine in that it takes time and work. It doesn't just arrive fully formed overnight: it evolves over years and it takes two, baby, as someone once sang.

When you agreed to take your wife for better, for worse and all that business, you also signed up to fulfil your obligation as a fine upstanding husband and follow each and every one of the unspoken Rules of Married Life. You might not remember agreeing to abide by the Rules, but you did. And there are loads of them; from the simple stuff at the start involving toilet seats and underpants, to the more complex business of DIY and, oh Lordy, life with the in-laws. It's a big job and a very steep learning curve, but luckily you've made the best possible start by picking up this very helpful tome. As the name suggests, *The Husbands' Book* will teach you every skill a husband will ever need.

Now, I could waffle on, but time is of the essence. Do yourself a favour and turn the page, my good man. The lessons are finally about to begin, and you've got a hell of lot to learn.

The Lore of the Rings: A Brief History of Grooms

The wedding day has always been one of the most significant days in a person's life so, understandably, over time the occasion has gathered various traditions and symbols; the wedding ring, the cake, the best man. But what is the significance of these often bizarre rituals?

The Stag Party

It is said that the stag party – or 'bachelor party' in North America, 'bull's party' in South Africa and 'buck's party' in Australia – was originally intended to ward off evil spirits before the wedding. These days, of course, it usually encourages spirits – of the alcoholic variety, that is. Another theory is that it originated with bachelor dinners that were traditional in Sparta in the fifth century BC, at which soldiers would toast each other on the eve of a friend's wedding.

It is thought that the bride's equivalent, the hen party, was introduced around the time of Charles II, in the seventeenth century, to allow the bride's friends and family to examine the trousseau, or 'bottom drawer': the fine linens that would form part of the bride's dowry.

The Best Man

In ancient times, men sometimes captured women to make them their brides: possibly not the best start to a loving, sharing marriage. A man would take along his strongest and most trusted friend to help him fight any resistance from the woman's family – in other words, he was the best man for the job. In Anglo-Saxon England, the best man accompanied the groom up the aisle to help defend the bride from similar resistance during the wedding ceremony. The tradition of the bride standing to the left of the groom at the altar, meanwhile, stems from the groom's need to keep his sword arm free. The stresses of the modern day wedding pale in comparison.

The Vows

The traditional marriage vows that promise to love 'for better or worse, for richer or poorer, in sickness and in health' come from the Form of Solemnization of Matrimony taken from the 1662 Book of Common Prayer. They have remained largely unchanged ever since.

In Hindu wedding tradition the vows take a different form, with the couple taking seven steps together, stating a verse with each one. After the seventh step, the groom says to the bride:

'With seven steps we have become friends. Let me reach your friendship. Let me not be severed from your friendship. Let your friendship not be severed from me.'

At Jewish weddings, the bride and groom walk down the aisle and stand beneath the *chuppah* (bridal canopy), an island of private holy space that symbolizes the Jewish home. Here the groom makes the declaration, 'You are consecrated to me, through this ring, according to the religion of Moses and Israel,' before giving the bride the ring. The ceremony concludes when the groom breaks a glass underfoot (thankfully wearing shoes).

The Ring

The placing of a ring by the groom onto the bride's finger originally had more to do with money than love. In Ancient Egypt, 'ring-money' (used prior to the introduction of coins) or hemp twisted into a ring, was put onto the bride's finger to indicate that she was now endowed with her husband's wealth.

The ring took on a more romantic significance in Ancient Greece. It was worn on the third finger of the left hand, because that particular finger was thought to contain a 'vein of love' leading directly to the heart.

In Roman times, a lady's acceptance of a ring was seen as a legally binding agreement, and a symbol that she was no longer available.

Back in the twelfth century, Pope Innocent III ordered that marriages be celebrated in church, and that the ceremony include a ring. Consequently, Christians adopted the wedding ring as a token of love and fidelity, and so it gained its religious significance.

The Cake

In Roman times, the groom would eat part of a loaf of barley bread, baked especially for the nuptials – and then break the rest over his bride's head! This symbolized the loss of the wife's virginity and the groom's consequent control of her. But as the cakes evolved into the more modern version we have today, they became too heavy to break over the bride's head, and so the practice ended.

The Toast

The now-essential 'toast' at wedding receptions began in France, where it was traditional to drop a small piece of toast into the couple's wine, to ensure a healthy life. They then lifted their glasses to a 'toast', as is common in Western culture today.

The Honeymoon

The origin of the word 'honeymoon' is a little uncertain. Some believe that it originated as an ancient Babylonian practice that involved drinking mead, a honey-based alcoholic drink, for a lunar month after marriage. Others claim that the word is actually a vulgarization of the Norse word *hjunottsmanathr*, meaning 'in hiding'. After the groom had kidnapped his bride, she was kept hidden away until she was either pregnant or her family had stopped looking for her, and then was brought back to formalize the wedding. How very romantic.

Weird Weddings

White dress and church? Best man and vicar? Congregation and confetti? At most western weddings, all of the above are usually present and correct. These are the very basic requirements of a traditional wedding, at least they used to be. Not any more. Weird developments are afoot, developments in which couples with a more maverick approach are saying no thank you to tradition and opting for a more 'individual' approach. One involving clowns, hamburgers, Elvis Presley and a vast tank of blood-thirsty sharks. You really couldn't make it up, only these crazy couples did . . .

'I Yabba-Dabba-Do'

Rick Sommers and Martine Tait ditched formal wedding attire for *Flintstones* fashion for their wedding. With his blond hair, Rick was perfect for the cartoon's Barney Rubble character and Martine was delighted to be his wife, Betty. Their best man and chief bridesmaid got in on the act as Fred and Wilma Flintstone and passers-by cheered and clapped as the four walked through Swindon town centre in their costumes. They'd kept their theme secret from everyone except the registrar so, when they finally arrived at the register office the stunned silence was soon broken by laughter.

It's a Mad World

Tony and Larisa Caplin can't stop getting married – to each other. The pair fly all around the world to tie the knot in different places and, so far, have wed five times in two years.

'We are mad about each other and one wedding was just not enough, so we are constantly dreaming up new ideas for marriage ceremonies,' explains Tony, from Kent. 'We want to cover the world and get married under every religion, because you can never have too many gods on your side.'

The pair first got hitched at Canterbury register office in Kent and have since had a Hindu ceremony on a beach in Goa; a Bedouin wedding in the Egyptian desert; a suitably Elvis-themed Las Vegas wedding; and finally a wedding in Larisa's hometown of Chelyabinsk, Russia.

'People think we're crazy but we're not; we're just in love and love getting married,' said Larisa.

'Eat In or Take Away?'

Family and friends were stunned when newly-weds Simon and Paula Hand left the register office in Cheshire and told everyone that the reception was being held at the McDonald's across the road.

'Nobody believed us, but we'd been planning it for months,' said Paula. Staff had decked out the upstairs section of the restaurant with balloons and laid on trays of Extra Value Meals.

The couple and twenty guests tucked into quarter-pounders, fries and chicken nuggets in a banquet that cost just £3.30 a head. After the speeches, they were toasted with a round of cokes and strawberry milkshakes!

'We wanted to do something different, but we didn't have a huge amount of money to spend,' said Paula. 'So it was value meals all round.'

Strong Attachment

Escapologist Dan Robinson made sure his wife Jackie didn't jilt him at the altar ... by handcuffing her to his side.

The bizarre wedding ceremony took place at Bournemouth register office and after the couple were pronounced man and wife, Dan picked the lock – being an escapologist he couldn't just use the key. But he wasn't finished there; at the wedding reception, Dan entertained the guests by escaping from a strait jacket and sticking an electric drill up his nose. Obviously.

That's All, Folks!

Cartoon fans Ruth Bunyard and Ian Carson dressed as Cinderella and Bugs Bunny for their wedding. Other guests turned up as Daffy Duck, Speedy Gonzales, Scooby Doo, Tweety Pie and Tom and Jerry for the ceremony at a Warner Brothers Studio store in Sheffield. You had to be there, really.

Send in the Clowns

Mark Powell felt a complete clown when he married his fiancée Lizzie. As well he might, given that both bride and groom were dressed in full clown outfits of outsized colourful clothes, curly wigs, gigantic shoes and big red noses.

The priest who married them joined in the fun by swapping his dog collar for a ringmaster's outfit, and the congregation also wore fancy dress, filling the church with medieval maids, Spanish dancers and even a Charlie Chaplin.

The couple left as man and wife to the tune of Rolf Harris's 'Tie Me Kangaroo Down, Sport'.

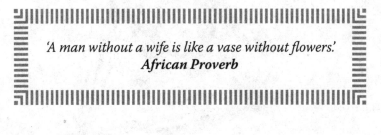

'A man without a wife is like a vase without flowers.'
African Proverb

Fish Wives

On their big day, keen scuba divers Nick Anderson and his wife-to-be, Judi Boon, took the plunge in a shark tank at Birmingham's National Sea Life Centre, surrounded by sharks, giant skate and other marine creatures. The couple from Bristol exchanged their vows underwater, through special microphones built into their helmets. The ceremony was taken by a minister standing outside the tank and watched from an underwater walkway by the couple's friends and family.

And when Gavin and Eileen Anderson wed in the safari tank at Deep-Sea World in North Queensferry, Scotland, the wedding vows were witnessed by seven sand tiger sharks and 3,500 other fish.

Dress or Sumo Outfit?

When Ryan Smallbone married his fiancée Melinda, the wedding guests included amongst their number Elvis, Zorro and the Pope.

The groom himself was transformed into an old woman in a scarf with a baby perched on his shoulders, for reasons inexplicable. Indeed, the only one not in fancy dress was the bride, who wore a striking full-length bridal gown, flown in from China.

'We got all the costumes off the internet,' said Ryan, from Essex. 'Melinda's dress was also from the internet and only arrived the day before the wedding. If it hadn't arrived in time, she was going as a sumo wrestler.'

Stealing Shoes

In Bengali weddings, the bride's younger relatives have to steal the groom's shoes, which he must remove before approaching the altar to be married. It's not just the bride's family that gets in on the fun, though – the groom's relatives have to try to hide his shoes from the would-be thieves. If they fail, however, the groom has to pay the successful thieves whatever sum they demand for the shoes' return!

Wedding Woes

A wedding day is a momentous occasion in any man's life, the day when months of planning come together with military precision to leave the bride and groom with tears in their eyes and memories to last them a lifetime. Well, that's the idea, in theory at least. But not all wedding days go quite according to plan. Consider the following examples, and be thankful that you weren't involved in any of these sorry episodes . . .

'Always get married in the morning. That way, if it doesn't work out, you haven't wasted the whole day.'
Mickey Rooney

The Full Monty

Gail O'Donnell and her husband Thomas were stunned when drunken yobs did a *Full Monty*-style strip in front of guests outside their reception. It was the final bum note in a sliding scale of disasters.

The day began badly when the reception hall in Lanarkshire was hit by a methane gas leak from a landfill site. Guests had to wait more than four hours as environmental health officers declared a full-scale alert and called in the fire brigade.

By the time the all-clear came, their chauffeur and the piper they'd paid to play at the reception had both gone.

'We also had to let the photographer go, along with coaches and cars that had been organized,' said Gail. 'I turned up in a Ford Fiesta and we had to flag down a bus off the street to ferry guests.'

As the evening's celebrations finally got underway, the band played the Tom Jones hit 'You Can Leave Your Hat On', which featured in the hit movie *The Full Monty*. But guests were shocked to see youths outside the window getting into the swing of things by stripping naked!

'We had to get the caretaker to bring down the shutters,' said Gail.

Frozen Out

The biggest day of Marianne and Joe Trovato's lives was booked for 12 February 1983, but they might have done well to check the weather forecast. Unfortunately their wedding coincided with the second-worst snowstorm ever to hit their home city of Philadelphia.

Nearly two feet of snow fell on the region. The church doors froze shut, the bridesmaids couldn't locate their cars under the blanket of white, and the roads were so precarious that the band was prohibited from driving to the reception by an emergency order from the State Governor. Eventually, the couple decided enough was enough and married a week later. 'A lot of people gave us free stuff,' said Joe. 'I think they felt sorry for us!'

Congratulations on Your ~~Wedding~~ Funeral

The omens were not good when Claire Nicols from Edinburgh looked out of her window on the morning of her big day to see not the white Rolls Royce festooned with ribbons that she'd been expecting, but a hearse. Two other funeral cars were parked nearby to transport other wedding party members. The hire firm admitted to an irate bride that there had been a mix-up, but said it was too late to make changes.

Thankfully the marriage service passed without a hitch, but when Claire and her husband Terry began to sign the register, the groom's brother rushed up to tell him a woman had fallen over in the aisle and was in too much pain to be moved. So, as the wedding march played, the newly-weds had to make their way towards the exit along the side of the congregation. Outside, as they were happily preparing for photographs, they were ushered aside by paramedics rushing up the steps – only to be pushed aside again moments later when the medics rushed out with the woman on a stretcher.

Terry and Claire were driven in the funeral car to the reception, where they discovered that their three-layered wedding cake wouldn't stand up because the glass pillars between the tiers were uneven.

After the meal, the couple was just standing up to greet the evening guests when a blue light flashed through the window. A fire engine had been called to put out a fire – but it turned out to be a hoax.

'It was a very memorable wedding,' said Claire, in something of an understatement.

Honeymoon Heaven, Honeymoon Hell

With the wedding over and all that planning behind you, it's time to relax and enjoy your eagerly anticipated honeymoon. It can be the happiest, most romantic time of your life, but be prepared, just in case things don't quite go according to plan. Below are some true stories of fairytale *and* nightmare honeymoons ...

Just the Two of Us

Sometimes keeping it simple is the key to romance. Journalist Rafael Behr and his wife thought of various exciting options for their honeymoon – a trip on the Orient Express, perhaps? Or a road trip in northern Spain? But in the end, after a stop-off in New York, they stayed in an isolated log cabin in New England, where it poured with rain and the fire wouldn't light. And they couldn't have been happier. He wrote in the *Observer*, 'We spent one rained-in afternoon doing a jigsaw puzzle. There were no paradise islands, no majestic herds of wildebeest, no cocktails. Just us with nothing much to do but hang out together. It was perfect.'

Busy Lady

The legendary wit Dorothy Parker had her honeymoon unceremoniously interrupted by her boss at *The New Yorker*, Harold Ross, demanding she submit a belated book review. Her terse reply? 'Too f***ing busy, and vice versa.'

Bride on Her Back

Catherine Jones, from Manchester, spent most of her honeymoon on her back – being carried across a desert on a stretcher!

She and her husband Ian chose to honeymoon by crossing the Atacama Desert in Chile on a seven-day, 150-mile charity challenge. It's the driest place on earth, with temperatures hitting a blistering 37°C during the day and dropping to well below freezing at night.

When Catherine, picked up a foot infection, she had to be carried on a makeshift stretcher – made from a folding chair and tent poles – by other competitors.

'People carried me on the stretcher and Ian got me over mountain passes on his back,' said Catherine. They eventually crossed the line with Catherine wearing a tiara, wedding veil and a 'Just Married' sign.

Swept Away by it All

Whirlwind romances are one thing but hurricanes are quite another. A few days after Arthur and Timi Morales arrived in St Croix, in the Virgin Islands, Hurricane Hugo struck, causing terrifying destruction.

'We didn't hear anything about the hurricane until our third day there,' said Arthur. By then, it was too late to move, and for the next five days hotel guests were forced to sleep on the floor, ration food and water and even make weapons as the tropical paradise turned into hell.

The hurricane overturned cars, ripped down trees and sent bricks flying through the air. The hotel's glass doors and windows were shattered. 'It scared the daylights out of us,' said Arthur. 'We thought we were going to die there.'

When the hurricane finally passed, they had no electricity, no running water and no aid. Hotel employees had given the twenty-six guests nine gallons of water, muffins, crisps and other packaged food, but it was fast running out.

'The last days we were very low on water and were drinking coconut milk,' said Arthur. Adding to their problems was the threat of looters, who hung around the hotel looking for easy pickings. Arthur, a police chief from California, had to fire a warning shot with one of the two guns that the beleaguered group had obtained from the hotel management. They also made weapons out of a sprinkler pipe for the women to carry.

'The only way we survived is that we stuck together until we were finally able to fly out,' said Arthur.

Surfer's Paradise

Pity the poor honeymooners who turned up at their exclusive hotel in Honolulu expecting the best … Having paid in excess of $1700 for a week's stay, the first thing the blissful couple were told was that the hotel operated a curfew that started at nine o'clock in the evening because of the dozens of prostitutes who tried to gain access after that time.

On being shown their suite, they found a small kitchen full of dirty dishes, and in the living rooms, wonky furniture covered in blankets to hide the stains and holes. In the bedroom there was a pair of shoes and a pile of clothes – and other 'unsightly' items under the bed. So distraught were they that they checked out immediately, only to be told that a hooker had probably broken in to the room – again. Classy.

Bad Hair Day

On his wedding night in 2004, a newly married university professor from Cairo was horrified to find that his bride's 'long voluminous hair' was not quite all it appeared to be. Having tied the knot the happy couple retired for the night and, after a while, the bride fell into a deep sleep, during which the aforesaid hair had slipped askew. She awoke to find her groom screaming and pointing at the now fallen locks in horror. The local newspaper reported that the professor said his thirty-four-year-old bride managed to fool him during the seven months they were engaged. He demanded an annulment and a waiving of any rights for the bride on the basis of her 'fraud and deception'. Let that be a lesson to us all.

Passport to Hell

A battered passport set off a disastrous chain of events for Chris and Margarita Webb of Cheshire. Arriving at Manchester Airport en route to Orlando, Chris was told that his passport was too tatty.

The passport was certainly well used – he had commuted weekly to Munich for the past two years – but he had never had a problem with it before. However, with heightened security at the airport, Chris had to travel to the passport office in Liverpool to get a new one. When he and his wife returned to Manchester Airport, they were told that the rearranged flight they had been promised did not exist. The only option was a flight the next day – from London.

When they eventually got to Florida, their hire car broke down fifteen minutes from the airport and their hotel had no record of any reservation!

The Learner Husband

As we've already established, being married is generally a bloody marvellous business, but it can often feel like being thrown in at the deep end for the new husband. Fret not, though, for that is quite natural. Unless you've cohabited with your other half beforehand and grown used to each other's little peculiarities, sharing your space with another person can be a disorientating business.

The biggest fear for any new husband is the supposed loss of independence that comes when you sign away your single status on that dotted line. Your life is no longer your own and from this day forth you'll never be free to leave your underpants in a pile in the corner of the bedroom, nor pass out on the sofa with kebab meat on your face. Nowadays, the new, improved, married you will have to consider your other half before you do absolutely anything. That's what marriage is about. If that thought sends a shiver down your spine, take comfort in the fact that she'll be feeling that very same shiver, and wondering what she's let herself in for. But rest assured, although it will take time to readjust to your new married life, as long as you're both flexible enough to adapt you'll not only survive but thrive and prosper.

To help you on your way, consider the following advice. It's by no means the definitive guide, but it should at least point you in the right direction.

The Learner Husband's Survival Guide

♦ Everyone needs their own space, even happily married couples. Just because you've tied the knot, that doesn't mean you have to be joined at the hip. Many men swear by a study or 'den', but if that seems a little extreme, a garage or shed makes for a more than acceptable bolt hole. And make sure your wife has a her own equivalent.

♦ Married life shouldn't put the kibosh on your social life. You can both still enjoy a night out with the boys/girls, but don't abuse it. The key, if you're clever, is to bring the two circles closer together, so that you socialize as a couple more, rather than in isolation. Obviously, this doesn't mean you should ditch your old friends just because you're now married, but that you include your wife in your plans wherever possible. The chances are she may not fancy discussing football's finer details in a grotty pub with you and your best man, but she'd certainly appreciate being asked along.

♦ Just because you share the house, you don't have to live in each other's pockets. Have your own hobbies and activities, such as football on a Sunday or a photography course in the week, and be happy that she has her own interests that don't include you. Opposites attract and make a relationship more interesting.

♦ Accept that there will be plenty of disagreements along the way, which is natural because you are two different people. But a discussion of ideas is one thing and a heated row involving four-letter words and flying crockery is quite another. If you feel the temperature rising, agree to disagree and swiftly move onto another topic. Cheese, for example. Everyone likes cheese.

♦ Remember that there are no rights or wrongs in a good marriage: just different ways of doing things. In time you'll learn that her way is indeed the more logical, but that doesn't make you wrong. Just less right.

'To keep your marriage brimming/ With love in the wedding cup,/ Whenever you're wrong, admit it;/ Whenever you're right, shut up.'
Ogden Nash

Things You Wished Your Father Had Told You

You may think you have had the last word,
but you never will.

Just because she's laughing doesn't mean she's happy.

Whatever way you do it, it wouldn't have been
the way she'd have done it.

When she says she has nothing to wear,
don't start listing items from her wardrobe.
She hasn't got anything to wear, okay?

One of you will always feel too hot while the other is too cold in bed.

The bathroom will be full of bottles, tubes and tubs of liquids and creams but you will have no idea what 80 per cent of them are for.

Shopping is a day out – not a chore.

The Art of Diplomacy

The truth and nothing but the truth should remain firmly inside the law courts. The most easy-going and innocent-sounding remark by your wife may turn out to be a ticking time bomb if you're not equipped with a suitable response. Coming up with one in a matter of seconds is no mean feat. So, to help you along the way, here are some we prepared earlier. (And of course it might be useful for your wife to learn these in reverse for when you need reassurance …)

She says: 'I need to go on a diet.'
You say: 'Okay, but don't go losing too much weight.'

She says: 'I look really rough.'
You say: 'You look as gorgeous as ever.'

She says: 'I feel old.'
You say: 'Old? You look ten years younger than you are.'

She says: 'Does my bum look big in this?'
You say: 'No, of course not. But I was hoping you were going to wear your sexy green outfit tonight. I love you in that.'

She says: '[Insert name of glamorous young actress] is gorgeous. Don't you think so?'
You say: 'Hmm … Okay, I suppose. A bit skinny/young for my liking.'

She says: 'Who would find me attractive?'
You say: 'All my friends, for a start.'

She says: 'I've got nothing to wear.'
You say: 'But it's all about style, and you always look better than the rest.'

She says: 'I bet you fancy [insert name of mutual female friend], don't you?'
You say: 'Why would I fancy her when I have you?'

She says: 'Do you like my new hair cut?'
You say: 'Yes!'

Husbands through History

For some husbands, the odd box of chocolates and a birthday card is enough to declare their undying love for their other halves. Other men, however, are prepared to go that extra mile, and should be an inspiration to us all …

Odysseus

The legendary Greek king of Ithaca, Odysseus, had to leave his wife Penelope when he went off to fight in the Trojan Wars, and was gone for twenty long years.

In his absence, Penelope was beset by suitors. But, although she was doubtful of ever seeing her husband again, she remained faithful to him, pretending to weave a burial shroud for Odysseus's dying father and stating that she could not take another husband until she had completed it.

Despite being ensnared by the enchantresses Circe and Calypso on his voyage home, Odysseus remained devoted to his wife and determined to return to her. When he finally made it back to his home he did so in disguise, and told Penelope that her husband had died.

Finally accepting her fate, she declared that whoever of her suitors could string his bow and shoot an arrow through twelve axe-handles would be her husband. Odysseus achieved this seemingly impossible feat, then slaughtered all the would-be suitors. We can't condone that, of course, but you take the point.

Pierre Abélard (1079 - 1142)

Abélard was a bright young academic who was appointed to lecture at the cathedral school of Notre Dame in Paris. He obtained lodgings with Canon Fulbert, who admired the young man's reputation. Then aged thirty-six, Abélard became tutor to Héloïse, the canon's beautiful seventeen-year-old niece. They began an affair but when Héloïse's uncle discovered them he threw Abélard out of the house. However, by this time Héloïse was pregnant and the couple fled to Brittany, where Héloïse gave birth to a baby boy. They returned with their son to Paris and married in secret.

Wedded bliss was not to be, however. One night, in an act of terrible revenge, some of Héloïse's outraged relatives broke into Abélard's room and castrated him. Though Abélard survived the attack, he insisted that his marriage to Héloïse be annulled, as he could no longer fulfil the duties of a husband. He became a monk and Héloïse was forced to take the veil, giving up her son to be adopted by her sister. Throughout this time, Héloïse and Abélard kept up a moving and passionate correspondence, which was published after their deaths around 1130. They are buried side by side at the Père Lachaise cemetery in Paris.

Prince Albert

The husband and consort of Queen Victoria had a significant influence on her as her husband and advisor. He also began to act as her private secretary and encouraged her to take a greater interest in social welfare.

They had nine children. When Albert died in 1861, Victoria was devastated. She did not appear in public for three years and never stopped mourning her beloved prince, wearing black until her death in 1901.

Prince Rainier

The fairytale romance of Prince Rainier of Monaco and film star Grace Kelly captivated the world. The pair met in May 1955, when Grace was attending the Cannes Film Festival and had agreed to be photographed with the prince for *Paris Match* magazine. There was an instant attraction and, after showing her around his gardens, they arranged a dinner date. That December, they announced their engagement and were married the following year.

Grace gave up her movie career to become Her Serene Highness Princess Grace of Monaco. After she was tragically killed in a car crash in September 1982, Prince Rainier was a broken man. He never fully recovered from her death and never re-married.

He died in April 2005, and was buried beside his wife, at Saint Nicholas Cathedral, Monaco.

Nicolas Sarkozy

The attention of the world's media was on the French president when he married the former supermodel and *femme fatale* Carla Bruni in 2008.

Both Sarkozy and Bruni have led colourful lives – Sarkozy's marriage to his previous wife, Cecilia, ended somewhat acrimoniously, with allegations of philandering on both sides; while Bruni's former lovers include infamous lotharios Eric Clapton, Vincent Perez, and the then very married Mick Jagger.

But Sarkozy demonstrated an important aspect of being a good partner – accepting your lover's past – when Carla admitted to him that some of her modelling jobs had been nude. Said Bruni, 'I took him aside and said: "I posed in the nude." He said: "Oh. Can I have a print?"'

Coping With the In-Laws

Meeting the in-laws for the first time (or the first few times) can bring even the most confident chap out in a bad case of the sweats. And with very good reason. The scenario is always the same for every would-be husband: you are a complete stranger to these people and you're here to be thoroughly vetted. They want to be assured that you're not some social misfit looking to get his hooks into their precious daughter. So you're here – most likely in their living room – to be looked up and down. You will be judged and your credentials thoroughly assessed by these people. However, you will probably be offered a glass or two of sweet sherry for your troubles, so it's not all bad.

Even so, you have every right to be nervous, because as someone or other once sagely opined, you never get a second chance to make a good first impression. Luckily, this is easily achieved if you don't get flustered and abide by the following five golden rules . . .

The Five Golden Rules

Rule 1: Be Yourself, But a Better Version

While it is important to remain true to the core of your personality, you can't just be your everyday self. You do have to make an effort. Don't try to be someone you're not, because that will be transparent and impossible to sustain, and do not, under any circumstances, attempt any impersonations. They will think you are weird and ask you to leave, and rightly so. Just think of your better qualities, work on them, and leave the rest behind.

Rule 2: Don't be Sycophantic

That means not making creepy comments such as telling your mother-in-law that you can see where her daughter got her looks from; laughing like a mad man at your father-in-law's jokes; and generally behaving like a wide-eyed puppy, scampering around trying to please its master.

Rule 3: Agree to Disagree

If you have made your point in a discussion with the in-laws, yet there is still some disagreement, let it lie. Don't go on and on like a dog with a bone. And don't raise your voice or be rude.

Rule 4: Don't Get Carried Away

This doesn't mean don't enjoy yourself, just be careful not to overdo the alcohol. And if you want to avoid the pitfalls, it may help to watch the film *Meet The Parents* – which is hilarious yet painful at the same time. Greg Focker (Ben Stiller) is so unnerved by girlfriend Pam's taciturn and vaguely threatening father Jack (Robert De Niro) that he can't relax – his garbled chat soon encompasses pot smoking and breast pumps. Remember this: if you find yourself in a hole, stop digging.

Rule 5: Shut Up and Listen

It's the safest thing to do. Don't be mute, of course, because that will freak them out. Do your bit to keep the conversation going and instigate conversations too, but know when to shut up. Everyone likes a good listener. Not everyone likes a good talker.

Abide by these five simple rules and you should make a very solid impression, which is the very least the in-laws are looking for. If you get past the first meeting and down the aisle with their daughter, you've obviously passed the test. Even so, you cannot now drop your guard and stop making the effort because, as the following sorry examples clearly illustrate, potential disaster lurks round every corner.

A Bum Deal

A wife's parents gave up their bedroom for her and her husband when they were visiting them. Prior to going to sleep, he was giving her a back massage as she lay on the bed, when her dad walked in to get something, forgetting to knock. He was greeted with the sight of the naked man, straddling his daughter! The next morning at breakfast, no one could make eye contact with each other and the next time they visited, they were put in the wife's sister's room.

Major Laugh

When his fiancée warned him that her father – a retired major in the army – pushed her previous boyfriend down the stairs after an argument, Tom was understandably nervous about meeting him. But, determined not to be intimidated, he handled dinner without causing any offence and, at the end of the night, said goodbye and addressed him, courteously, as 'Sir'.

'You can call me Mr McCormack,' he replied, shaking Tom's hand. Without thinking, Tom cheekily replied, 'Great, you can call me Mr Andrews.' There was a brief silence, as his fiancée looked at him, nervously, and Tom began to look for his escape route. But, much to his relief, the major laughed. His comment had broken through the formality of the occasion and Tom was gladly accepted into the family when he got married.

Sick with Nerves

Newly-wed Paul was so nervous during dinner with his in-laws that he drank rather too much red wine at the table. As he started to relax, he began chatting a lot more, becoming louder, until he was really quite enjoying himself and thinking what a nice couple they were. At the end of the evening, he stood up, swayed, and had to be helped to an armchair. His embarrassed wife then watched in horror as he was sick all over his lap and the floor. Paul has never been able to put the incident out of his mind because every time he visits, he still sees a stain on the carpet where he disgraced himself.

A Bubbly Character

The first time he ever stayed with his in-laws, Greg took a bath the following morning and was delighted to see that it was a whirlpool one, where you press a button to activate jets of water. He lay back as the bath was filling up with water and added some bubble bath. But he put so much in that when he turned on the jets, the foam rapidly increased until it started flowing down the sides of the bath and across the floor! A panicky Greg stood up and started ladling out handfuls of foam into the bathroom sink. He flushed some more of it down the toilet and mopped the floor, which finally controlled the situation.

The Incompetent's Guide to DIY

By all means, get the professionals in when it comes to repairs and improvements around the house. A good plasterer, for instance, is worth his weight in gold – knocking down walls is definitely not a job for the amateur. But a good partner needs to be able to do some DIY, even if it's just unblocking the loo or changing a fuse. Follow these step-by-step guides and not only will you impress others but you too will be pretty darn chuffed with your achievements.

How to Unblock a Loo

This is one of those tasks that, while not a whole heap of fun, earns you great credit if you complete it successfully. You will need:

♦ Heavy-duty rubber gloves
♦ That useful implement, a straightened-out wire coat hanger (you can retain the hook at the end)
♦ A large sink plunger
♦ A bucket and access to a cold-water tap
♦ A heavy-duty rubbish bag, which must be waterproof (not a carrier bag – these often have air holes punched in them)
♦ Mind and nostrils closed to the noisome task ahead

▶ Lavatories almost always get blocked in the bend (known as the 'foul-water trap' or 'S-bend') behind the bowl. (To check this, run some water into the bath and washbasin, then let the plugs out. If the water doesn't run out, then the waste – or outlet – pipe is blocked further down. Probably time to call a plumber, in that case.) They are generally blocked by wadded masses of loo paper (children excel at this), other objects that shouldn't be put down loos anyway, and what plumbers, who seem to have a liking for euphemism, call 'heavy deposits' . . .

▶ Don't keep flushing the loo, hoping the obstruction will shift. If it isn't shifting, all that will happen is that the bowl will fill up, and may eventually overflow.

▶ Try to avoid using strong chemicals such as caustic soda or proprietary drain unblockers. They won't necessarily have much effect on a mass of wadded paper; they're nasty stuff to get on your skin or in your eyes, or if you inhale the gases they give off on contact with water; and they're really bad for the environment.

▶ Lift the seat and seat lid, don the gloves, take a deep breath and reach into the bowl to seize a handful of whatever's obstructing the outlet. Throw the result into the bin bag, and repeat the operation until you can reach no further. Now take the straightened-out hanger, bend it so that the hook end can reach into the outlet at the bottom of the bowl, and haul out as much more of the obstruction as you can; if that's not possible, use the straight end of the hanger to break up the blockage. Dispose of anything you pull out in the bin bag. Now insert the plunger and 'plunge' vigorously several times – this should 'blow' the rest of the obstruction down the waste pipe. Next, fill the bucket with clean cold water (from the bath tap, perhaps) and pour it down the bowl in one go (trying not to let it overflow or splash). This should have cleared the obstruction, and you can clean up, seal the bin bag and throw it away, and wash the tools (and your hands and arms) with a solution of disinfectant. Then flush the loo again, to make sure that all is now well. Announce triumph to your wife, who will be properly grateful, even if she does wrinkle her nose at the powerful reek of disinfectant.

▶ If this doesn't work, and the obstruction remains, you will need a set of flexible drain rods with a rubber disc that screws on to one end and acts as a plunger. However, if you're now getting into buying plumbing equipment that with any luck you won't use more than once every five years, it's probably time to call a plumber instead.

▶ If there is no visible blockage in the bowl or the bend, try using the plunger or, if desperate, caustic soda or proprietary drain unblocker. (If you decide to use the latter, wear heavy-duty rubber gloves, and follow the instructions very, very carefully.) This may indicate that the blockage is further down the waste pipe, which in turn may mean that you'll have to follow the drain-rod/plumber route . . .

REMEMBER: never put anything down the bowl that isn't either loo paper or 'human waste' – it's asking for trouble.

How to Replace a Fuse in a Fuse Board

> **IMPORTANT:** before changing any fuse, find what has caused it to blow – usually either a short-circuit or an overload – and correct the fault. Otherwise, the fuse will simply blow again.

YOU WILL NEED:
a screwdriver of the correct size and type
fuse wire of the correct rating (5, 10 or 15 amp)

Modern domestic electrical circuits no longer use replaceable fuses, but rely on circuit breakers; if one of these is tripped (the equivalent of a blown fuse), the cause must be discovered and put right, and then the circuit breaker can be reset.

Many buildings, however, still have older fuse boards incorporating removable fuses (properly, fuse-holders) in which a circuit is completed by a length of fuse wire running between two terminals. (If a fuse blows, it will usually be in a lighting circuit, since sockets are protected by fused plugs on appliances.)

If a main fuse has blown, check what has caused the problem and rectify it, then go to the fuse board and turn off the main power switch (which is usually clearly marked with 'ON' or 'OFF', depending on which position the switch is in). Then take off the cover over the fuses by loosening the captive screw that secures it. If you're lucky, each fuse will be identified as to which part of the circuit it serves (e.g. 'Bedroom 2 & landing'); if not, you will have to remove each fuse in turn and examine them to see in which one the fuse wire has blown.

Once identified, slacken the two screws securing the fuse wire and remove the two ends (two, because the wire will have separated in the middle when it blew), then insert a length of the correct rating fuse wire (5 amp is the thinnest, 15 amp the thickest) – i.e. of the same rating as the blown fuse – into the fuse-holder, wind each end around each terminal screw, and tighten the screws.

Replace the fuse-holder and then the cover, then turn on the main switch once more. If you fixed the original problem that caused the fuse to blow, that part of the circuit should now work again.

> **REMEMBER:** electricity is extremely dangerous, and can be lethal. If you are at all unsure about replacing a fuse, call an electrician or seek expert advice.

How to Slacken Wheel Nuts

You are driving with your wife when you suffer a puncture. Having pulled safely off the road, you realize that here is your chance to show some manly qualities by changing the wheel. The only problem is, when the car was last serviced the wheels were replaced by a mechanic using a pneumatic or electric spanner with the torque setting turned up too high. Result: wheel nuts that can't be budged with the wheel brace provided with the car . . . Furious wife insists you call the breakdown service . . . Utter humiliation.

There are two answers to this problem, given that the wheel braces provided with all but the most expensive cars are usually too short to allow much leverage to be exerted, that mechanics often overtighten the nuts, and that the threads are often rusty and clogged with road grit, making it harder to slacken or turn the nuts.

▶ The first is: keep a two-foot length of strong steel tubing just wide enough to fit over the wheel-brace handle in the boot with the jack and brace. This will allow you to exert far greater leverage on the overtightened nut, making it much easier to slacken. Be careful when using it to retighten the nuts, though, as the extra leverage may cause you to overtighten them, or even to strip the threads.

▶ The second is: buy a socket spanner head of exactly the correct size for the wheel nuts, as well as a 6-inch extension bar and a T-bar with which to turn the socket and extension. Keep it in the boot with the other tools – it will make slackening the wheel nuts much easier. And if they're badly overtightened, you can always use your length of steel tubing on the T-bar.

IMPORTANT: always make sure that the socket or wheel-brace head fits the nut tightly and squarely. If the head of the nut becomes damaged because the spanner slips, then it will have to be removed by a specialist and replaced.

An Easy Dinner to Impress

We all like to be cooked for, but some husbands don't even try to impress their wives in the kitchen. Even if you don't know a wok from a spatula, here is a three-course meal that's easy to prepare and quick to make, but that is guaranteed to impress.

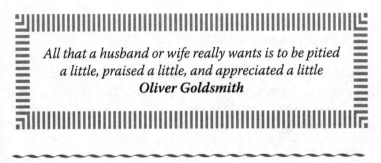

All that a husband or wife really wants is to be pitied a little, praised a little, and appreciated a little
Oliver Goldsmith

Starter

CARROT AND LENTIL SOUP

INGREDIENTS:
1 tablespoon oil
1 onion, chopped
2 carrots, chopped
85g/3oz split red lentils
1 litre/2 pints vegetable stock
1 teaspoon dried coriander
salt and pepper
plain yoghurt
parsley, finely chopped to garnish

▶ Step 1: Heat the oil in a large saucepan. Add the onion and carrots and fry for 3–5 minutes over a low heat until softened.

▶ Step 2: Rinse the lentils in cold water and add them to the pan, along with the stock and coriander, and bring to the boil. Lower the heat, cover and simmer gently for 30 minutes or until the lentils are tender, stirring occasionally.

▶ Step 3: Add salt and pepper to taste, then pour into a processor and blend until smooth.

▶ Step 4: Ladle into soup bowls, add a dollop of yoghurt into each and give a quick swirl with a knife. Sprinkle a little parsley over each and serve with wholemeal, brown or malted grain bread or roll.

Main Course

STEAK WITH RED WINE SHALLOTS AND CHUNKY CHIPS

INGREDIENTS:

FOR THE CHIPS:
3 large potatoes
vegetable oil, for deep frying

FOR THE MEAT AND SHALLOTS :
25g/1oz butter
2 shallots, finely chopped
1 large glass red wine
150ml/¼ pint beef stock
1 tablespoon olive oil
2 sirloin steaks

▶ Step 1: Peel the potatoes and cut into chip-sized pieces – about ½ in (1cm) square by 3in (7cm) long.

▶ Step 2: Fill a deep-fat fryer or a large, deep pan two-thirds full with vegetable oil and heat until hot. NEVER leave it unattended. Carefully place the chips into the hot oil and cook for about 8 minutes, until golden and half-cooked.

▶ Step 3: Remove the chips from the oil with a slotted spoon. Keep the oil in the pan but turn the heat down low. Drain the chips on kitchen paper.

Now it's time to make the red wine sauce and the steaks, before finishing off the chips at the end.

▶ Step 4: Melt the butter in a pan and gently cook the shallots for about 3 minutes, without browning.

▶ Step 5: Add the red wine and stock and cover. Bring to the boil, then simmer.

▶ Step 6: While the sauce is cooking, heat a frying pan, wipe with some olive oil, season the steaks on both sides with salt and pepper, and sear them, without moving them around, until a nice light-brown crust appears on the meat. Turn the meat and cook the other side (about 1–2 minutes on each side for rare steak, 3 minutes for medium and 4 minutes for well done).

▶ Step 7: Remove the steaks from the pan and allow them to rest in a warm place while you cook the chips a second time.

▶ Step 8: Increase the temperature of the chip-pan oil until hot. Gently add the cooked chips to the oil and fry for 2–3 minutes or until crisp and golden. Remove from the oil using a slotted spoon and drain on kitchen paper.

▶ Step 9: Place each steak onto a plate, ladle the sauce over each and serve with the chunky chips.

Vegetarian Option

SPAGHETTI VESUVIUS

INGREDIENTS:
1 tablespoon olive oil
400g/14oz tin plum tomatoes
1 teaspoon dried oregano
115g/4oz mozzarella cheese
25g/1oz freshly grated Parmesan cheese
250g/9oz spaghetti

▶ Step 1: Warm the oil in a large saucepan. Add the tomatoes, squashing them in the pan with a fork. Add the oregano. Cook rapidly for 20 minutes until you have a thick sauce.

▶ Step 2: Meanwhile, dice the mozzarella into small cubes and grate the Parmesan.

▶ Step 3: Cook the spaghetti in another large pan of water, following the instructions on the packet (usually boil for around 11 minutes or until *al dente* – firm and neither too hard nor too soft). When it is ready, drain well and add the Parmesan, keeping just a little back. Toss so that the Parmesan coats the spaghetti. Add the tomato sauce and the diced mozzarella. Toss rapidly, cover and leave for 3–5 minutes until the mozzarella melts to resemble a stream of molten lava (Vesuvius – get it?).

▶ Step 4: Give the mixture a stir and dish out onto plates or bowls. It is messy to serve so make sure you have plenty of kitchen roll to wipe clean the edges of the plates before serving with a side salad. Place the remainder of the Parmesan cheese on the table so that it can be sprinkled on top, if required.

Dessert

BLACKBERRY HONEY DELIGHTS

INGREDIENTS:
250g/9oz Greek yogurt
2 tablespoon runny honey
175g/6oz blackberries
half a cup of blackberry coulis
handful of crushed gingernut biscuits

▶ Step 1: Beat the yoghurt and honey together in a bowl.

▶ Step 2: Divide half the berries between two glasses, drizzle with some coulis and spoon over the yogurt. Sprinkle the gingernut biscuits on top. Add the rest of the berries and some coulis. Serve chilled.

Celebrity Marriages

Yes, celebrities experience the very human aspects of marriage too – here are some amusing, and some touching, anecdotes of famous couplings.

That's pukka!

When TV chef Jamie Oliver was wooing his wife, Jools, as a teenager, she told *Red* magazine, 'He worked double shifts at his dad's pub, from 6a.m. to 1a.m., and saved up £2,000 to take me to Greece. Most boys of seventeen wouldn't do that kind of thing, but that's just what he's like.' Aww, bless.

TomKat

It has been one of the most intensely scrutinized relationships of all time, but there's no denying that Tom Cruise knows how to romance his lady, Katie Holmes. He wooed her the traditional way by proposing in the early hours one morning on the Eiffel Tower; then subjected himself to the world's ridicule by jumping up and down on Oprah's couch, all in the name of love.

We Wannabe Together

Despite various rumours to the contrary, it seems the institution that is the Beckhams' marriage seems as solid as ever. Compromise obviously plays a big part in making their partnership work, with Victoria stating, 'I know I would sacrifice anything for my boys [David and her sons], including my career, even though I also know that they would never ask me to.' And for his part, David kicks those pesky tabloid gossips into touch, saying 'People can say what they like. But me and Victoria will always stay together as husband and wife.' So back off, ladies.

Enduring Love

Daytime TV's favourite married couple, Richard Madeley and Judy Finnegan, have been together for over a quarter of a century – an impressive fact that Madeley attributes to ... sex. 'Sex is the bedrock for me,' he told the *Observer*. 'Some people say a passionate physical relationship isn't important. I think they're in denial. I don't mean there's hot action every night down Hampstead way, but there's a fundamental physical attraction.' Too much information, Richard, too much information.

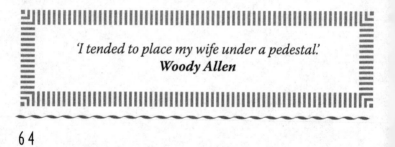

'I tended to place my wife under a pedestal.'
Woody Allen

The Perfect Valentine's Day

We'll get onto the perfect Valentine's Day in due course, but first . . .

> *'Love is composed of a single soul inhabiting two bodies.'*
> **Aristotle**

A Word of Warning

It's 14 February, so what, my hot-blooded friend, could be more romantic than showing just how much love you have coursing through your veins by following the same horribly forced tradition as every other male in the western world on the exact same day?

- Overpriced Valentine's Day card? ☑
- Overpriced cheap red roses? ☑
- Overpriced table for two in a dimly-lit restaurant full of other tables for two? ☑
- Same look of mild disappointment you received last year? ☑

The point of romance, as any doting husband should have learnt long ago, is that it doesn't just pop up on 14 February every year. Romance is a full-time job. Cupid never sleeps. Or if he does it's only ever for a few hours a night while he recharges his batteries.

Now the point we're perhaps labouring here is that romance should be spontaneous. It should turn up unannounced and surprise her, sweep her off her feet while simultaneously keeping her on her toes. Anyway, here endeth the Word of Warning. On with the entry.

The Perfect Valentine's Day

The gestures and advice detailed here will have far more impact if sprinkled throughout the year, rather than on the one day of the year when she's fully expecting it. Far better to surprise her for no obvious reason and when she least expects it. However, if you are celebrating Valentine's Day with everyone else, the following advice will stand you in good stead.

The Flowers

Don't purchase cheap, wilting carnations from the petrol station on your way home from work. She's worth a damn sight more than £3.49, is she not? Roses are a traditional symbol of affection, but azaleas, tulips and violets are all equally romantic and show you've given it some real thought. If you really want to earn extra brownie points, find out what her favourite flowers are and get her a bunch of those instead.

The Card

What could be less romantic than a card featuring a romantic ode written by a jobbing card designer in a factory on some business park in the middle of nowhere? The card should come blank and the only words within it should be penned by you and should come from the heart and in legible handwriting, rather than some hasty scrawl. If you have to opt for a card with a message already included, make sure any humour is subtle and sweet rather than smutty or vulgar.

Also, posting the card anonymously, as from a mystery admirer, is a nice idea – but tread carefully. A friend of a friend once forgot to stick a stamp on his card, and so, when the postman arrived on Valentine's Day, the dolt's wife opened the door to be presented with her card – plus a bill for the postage. Which kind of took the edge off things.

So, you have flowers, you have a card, but you know full well that these are merely the basics, the very least she deserves. The following suggestions are additional flourishes that should make all the difference.

Breakfast in Bed

Arise uncharacteristically early, cook up an imaginative breakfast and bring it to her in bed on a tray, along with your card and flowers, and a glass of buck's fizz (see p. 70).

HOW TO PREPARE THE PERFECT EGGS BENEDICT

INGREDIENTS:
For the hollandaise sauce:
150ml/5fl oz dry white wine
225ml/8fl oz white wine vinegar
15 whole black peppercorns
3 egg yolks
250g/9oz unsalted butter, cubed
lemon juice

For the eggs Benedict:
2 eggs
2 English muffins, sliced in half, toasted
4 slices ham

▶ Step 1: For the hollandaise sauce, put the white wine, white wine vinegar and black peppercorns into a heavy-based pan over a medium heat. Bring to the boil and reduce the liquid in the pan to half its original volume.

▶ Step 2: Strain the reduced mixture into a heatproof glass bowl. Add the egg yolks, with one small cube of the butter. Set over a pan of gently simmering water and whisk until slightly thickened.

▶ Step 3: Whisk in the remaining butter, a few cubes at a time, until it is all incorporated and you have a good thick sauce. The sauce needs to be warm. If you think it's too hot, take the pan and bowl off the heat and continue. Whisk in a good squeeze of lemon juice.

> **TIP:** If the sauce curdles, it is too hot. Drop an ice cube into the sauce and whisk again to re-emulsify. Once properly emulsified, the sauce will remain stable, giving you time to prepare the rest of the dish.

▶ Step 4: To poach the eggs, fill a pan with water. Bring to the boil and make a 'whirlpool' in the pan by swirling a spoon around the edge of the pan. Carefully crack the eggs into the pan, in the centre of the whirlpool. Poach the eggs until the whites are firm but there's still movement in the yolk.

▶ Step 5: To serve, place half a grilled muffin on a plate. Top with a slice of ham, the other muffin half and another slice of ham. Carefully remove the poached eggs from the pan and place on top of the ham. Spoon the hollandaise sauce on top and around the muffins and serve immediately.

Buck's fizz

Buck's fizz is the perfect accompaniment to eggs Benedict – light, refreshing and easy to concoct; just pour one part orange juice to two parts champagne.

Places to Go

The theatre, cinema or opera are all traditional places for couples to go for Valentine's Day, as is a romantic restaurant where you'll pay extra for the dim lighting. For 'traditional', however, you could also read 'obvious', so expect to be jostled for position by like-minded couples. If you're feeling slightly more intrepid and want all of the above but in a language you don't fully understand, head for a weekend in Paris, the epicentre of all things suave, sophisticated and utterly romantic, but every bit as busy as back home. Or book a pod just for the two of you on the London Eye and take a picnic with champagne. If all of the above sounds far too overcrowded ever to be romantic, there is an alternative: stay at home …

A Cosy Day Indoors

On any other day, sitting around at home would be considered a waste of precious time, but not on Valentine's Day, when you can spend all day enjoying just being together.

If 14 February falls on a weekday, all the better; you can both take the day off – it will feel all the more decadent. Surprise your wife by secretly booking the day off for her, via a friend on the inside who can fill out the relevant paperwork. How you fill your day will then be determined by your imagination. But if you're drawing a blank, consider the following …

♦ Rise early, bound down to the newsagent and stock up on her favourite magazines and the day's papers. Add freshly baked pastries and some fresh coffee, then rush home and get back under the duvet to enjoy your treats. And no, that's not a cheap smutty reference, though it easily could be.

♦ When you finally decide to get out of bed, start the day with a treasure trail by hiding small Valentine's gifts for her around the house, which she can find by solving clues that relate to your life together. Depending on the depth of your pockets/imagination, this game can be stretched out throughout the day, with the surprises waiting at every turn.

♦ If you're big on nostalgia, spend the morning looking through old photographs together – ones of your wedding, old holidays you've spent together, or ones of both of your childhoods. It's a good way to remember special moments you've shared, and to re-connect.

◆ Pack a romantic picnic and head for the garden if it's sunny, or the sofa in the lounge if it's not (and bearing in mind it's 14 February, don't get your hopes up). You don't have to go to a park to have a picnic – make up a hamper the day before with bits and pieces from your local delicatessen and bakers, spread out a blanket and have a nice lazy lunch. Consider adding wine, too, providing it's after 11a.m.

◆ Play a game in the afternoon – cards if either of you know how to play, or favourite board games from your childhood. Twister, perhaps, if you're still flexible enough and can get back up once it's over.

◆ Don't flick that TV switch! Watching a film is allowed, particularly if it's an old favourite and particularly if it's in black and white, which somehow makes it more acceptable, but don't just sit and watch anything that's on the box. This is time for the two of you, and you can't be giving each other proper attention if you're staring at the snooker all day.

◆ And as for the evening, well, that's really none of our business . . .

An Offbeat Day

If the traditional approach seems a bit run-of-the-mill for your liking and you're an adventurous, outdoors, fun-loving type, here are several suggestions that will set pulses racing. Literally.

Go-karting: Get an adrenaline rush by competing against each other on a go-kart track.

Bowling alley: Strike it right with a fun day spent ten-pin bowling.

Hot-air balloon: The sky's the limit with a romantic flight in a hot-air balloon, but make sure neither of you has vertigo first ...

Clay-pigeon shooting: Enjoy the sophisticated sport of shooting, without having to actually kill a living creature.

Indoor mountaineering: Keep warm and cosy while still enjoying the challenge of climbing.

Real-life Romeos

Who says romance is dead? There are still a few modern-day Romeos around to prove that a combination of love, imagination and planning will have hearts melting. Here are some touching examples of romance in action – as well as one romantic gesture that didn't quite work out as planned ...

Personal Romantic Movie

When Tina Kilford went to watch a film at her local Dorset cinema with some friends, she was stunned to see her boyfriend as the star.

As the movie began, love-struck Tom Lane appeared on screen, dressed in a dinner jacket, and proceeded to hold up a series of flashcards expressing his devotion to his girlfriend. Drawing his inspiration from Bob Dylan, he revealed twenty-three short messages until he reached 'Will You Marry Me?' The final card in the three-minute film, accompanied by Joe Cocker's 'You Are So Beautiful', read 'I'm right behind you.' Tina turned to see him standing there and immediately said 'Yes', and the audience burst into applause.

Tom had spent six weeks planning the big-screen proposal. 'It was a military operation,' he said. 'I am a ridiculous romantic but I wasn't hundred per cent sure she would say yes.'

Soul Mate

Christine Fearns knew her boyfriend was her soulmate when he proposed to her in front of her favourite actor.

When Paul Normington heard that Christine's hero, David Soul, was starring in the play *Mack and Mabel* at their local theatre in Darlington, he wrote to him and arranged for his girlfriend of three years to meet the *Starsky and Hutch* actor at an after-show party.

A delighted Christine had another surprise in store when Paul got down on one knee and proposed with a diamond and sapphire ring.

'It was the most romantic thing I have ever done,' said Paul.

Be My Juliet

After a performance of *Romeo and Juliet* at the Playhouse Theatre in Vancouver, the 700-strong audience was treated to a real life marriage proposal from James Milacic to Monita Raj.

James had been planning the surprise for three weeks, with the help of the theatre manager. He pre-ordered a dozen red roses to be presented to Monita after the proposal and persuaded her brothers and sister to get tickets to the performance, without them knowing his intentions.

After the curtain call, one of the actors gave a short speech about love and invited James onto the stage. Once there, he faced a stunned Monita, sitting in the front row, and proposed to her. She walked up to join her fiancé on stage and said 'Yes' as the crowd cheered and clapped.

In a Field of His Own

Farmer's son James Andrews, of Norfolk, decided to pop the question to his girlfriend by having the message 'Floss, marry me?' ploughed into a field in 165ft-high letters.

He persuaded Floss Allen to take an impromptu flight over the family farm to give her a bird's-eye view of his giant proposal. When she saw the message – the handiwork of James's father – she burst into tears and agreed to marry him.

Treasure Trail

A treasure trail is not just for kids. It can be exciting for adults, too, as Kirrily Gately found out.

One afternoon, she received a mysterious text message that said: 'Go to the florist in Martin Place.' Feeling a little foolish, she nevertheless went along and introduced herself and was presented with a huge bouquet of red roses with a small card attached. The card said: 'Now go to the Darrell Lea shop in George Street.' Here she was given a bag of assorted chocolates and yet another card that read: 'Go to the Forbes Hotel and ask for Emma the barmaid.' Emma the barmaid gave her a six-pack of lager and a final note telling her to get into a taxi and go to a certain bench in the park.

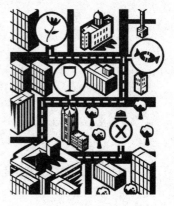

Waiting for her in the park was her boyfriend, Greg, who had set up a magnificent picnic on the grass overlooking Sydney Harbour. As she got out of the taxi, he dropped to one knee, presented her with a stunning ring and asked her to marry him. The dewy-eyed Kirrily was only too delighted to accept.

Tattoo Much

Sadly, the grand gesture doesn't always work. So be prepared …

After fifteen happy years with his wife, Alan Jenkins from Wales decided it was time for the ultimate expression of love. Determined to prove his devotion, he had a life-sized image of her face – along with those of their two daughters – tattooed on his back. The painful procedure took twenty hours and cost £870. But all that suffering for art was wasted after thirty-six year old Lisa absconded with a twenty-five-year-old Latvian hunk she had met at work.

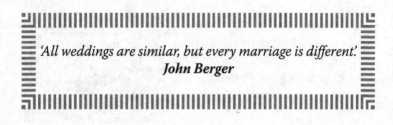

'All weddings are similar, but every marriage is different.'
John Berger

Show Her You Care

10 Ways to be the Best Husband:

1. Surprise her with a night out at a restaurant – without it being a 'special' occasion.

2. Play with the kids or take them out somewhere so that she can have some time to herself at home, alone.

3. While she's out, clean the house so that she returns to a nice clean home.

4. Buy her flowers – for no particular reason.

5. Decorate the house how she wants it.

6. Suggest that she invite her parents/family over for dinner – and be nice to them!

7. Compliment her on the way she looks – husbands don't do this half as much as they should.

8. Suggest that she has a night out with her friends, without it being an excuse for you to go on the lash with yours.

9. If she's feeling stressed, treat her to a relaxing massage.

10. Never forget the importance of saying, 'I love you'.

The Fashion Guru

When it comes to women's fashion, most husbands don't know their A-line from their empire waist. Wives know this, of course. But every now and then, they will suddenly ask your advice on the subject as if you are a cross between Christian Dior and Giorgio Armani. The exchange is usually brief, along the lines of:

Wife: 'Do you think this top goes with this skirt?'
Husband: 'Er ... Yeah.'

Then, having come to her senses once more and remembered that you are to fashion what Homer Simpson is to academia, she will not ask your advice again for another month or two. And so it goes on.

But what if you could actually make an informed reply? Imagine her shock and delight when you come over all Ralph Lauren with just a hint of Alexander McQueen. The secret to being an instant fashion guru is know the names of a few styles and to link them with a sprinkling of 'industry' words to form a convincing sentence. And here's the beautiful thing – most of it can be complete nonsense because it's not what you know, it's how you say it.

So take a look at this handy glossary, practise some of our ready-made phrases and do a bit of mix-and-match from time to time, and you'll have everything sewn up, so to speak.

Glossary

A–line: Skirt or dress that flares away from the bust or waist to make an 'A' shape.

Asymmetric: Uneven or one-sided, non-symmetrical. Hemlines may be diagonal or tops have just one shoulder strap or sleeve.

Boot-cut: Trousers where the leg gently flares from the knee to become wider at the hem.

Broderie anglaise: Stitching technique in which small patterns are cut out of a white fabric and the edges overstitched, also in white, creating delicate designs used most often in underwear and trimmings for dresses.

Cap sleeve: Short sleeve popular on a blouse or dress that only extends over the top of the shoulder.

Court shoe: Medium-heeled, often pointed shoe, with low-cut front and no fastening.

Cowl: Fabric that hangs in soft folds, often found on necklines and backs.

Culottes: Flared knee-length trousers cut full, to look like a skirt

Décolleté: Very low-cut neckline that bares the shoulders.

Empire waist: A waistline that is pushed up to just below the bust. First popularized during the 1800s in France by Napoleon's wife, Empress Josephine.

Halter-neck: Dress or top tied around the neck with a single strap, exposing the back and shoulders.

Kitten heel: Shoe with a low, tapered heel that is set slightly forward.

Pedal pushers: Tight trousers that fall below the knee.

Pencil skirt: Knee-length skirt cut straight and close-fitting.

Ruche/Ruched (pronounce roosh/rooshed): fabric gathered and sewn into a seam shorter than the length of the fabric, forming ruffles. Often used for trim.

Slingback: Backless shoe with a rear strap that goes around the upper heel, usually with a buckle.

Spaghetti straps: Very fine, ribbon-like dress straps, popular on summer dresses.

Tankini: A swimsuit combining a tank top with a bikini bottom.

Wedge: Shoe with a one-piece sole that is shaped like a wedge. Often open-toed and open-backed.

Ready-made phrases

Wife: Does this top go with this skirt?
Husband: The russet brown and the forest green provide a perfect autumnal coordination.

Wife: What shoes do you think I should wear with these trousers?
Husband: While kitten-heels add just the right feminine touch to a trouser suit, I would suggest booties or court shoes for trousers alone.

Wife: I think this dress might be a bit low-cut for the occasion.

Husband: But the décolleté is exquisitely tailored to enhance your swan-like neck.

Wife: I don't know what skirt to wear.

Husband: The charcoal pencil-skirt is made for your slender hips, and combines sexiness with an understated confidence and timeless elegance.

Wife: Does the light blue goes with the pale yellow?

Husband: The pastel palette is perfect for the season.

Wife: What do you think of this top?

Husband: The cut is beautifully flattering and the cowl neck provides a canvas for a delicate necklace to complete the look.

Wife: Is this too young for me?

Husband: No – the elegant lines, combined with the fluted cap sleeves and tiered hemline combines childlike simplicity with grown-up glamour.

Ghastly Gifts

When buying presents, it's best to remember those occasions when you've been bought gifts that made your heart sink. Don't buy what you think you would like to receive – think carefully about what she likes, and be imaginative. No one likes to be able to anticipate what they're going to get.

Scenarios to avoid:

He thinks: Hmm ... Sexy red undies.
She thinks: I'm not wearing those tacky things.

He thinks: She likes to work out. I know! An exercise DVD.
She thinks: He thinks I'm fat.

He thinks: I'll buy her some of that expensive anti-wrinkle cream she likes.

She thinks: So, I'm looking old and lined.

He thinks: Garden vouchers. She loves pottering around outside.

She thinks: Has he no imagination whatsoever?

He thinks: A beautiful paperweight to keep her papers tidy.

She thinks: Doorstop.

He thinks: A CD compilation of charts hits.

She thinks: I only like two tracks on this.

He thinks: Slippers.

She thinks: He doesn't fancy me any more.

Perfect Presents

So now you know what not to do, here are a few ideas that are guaranteed to make her happy . . .

What She Actually Wants (For Once)

As we've already suggested, it's all too easy to buy your wife something she doesn't actually want. A 'Goals of the Season' box set, for example, or tool set with a retractable work bench. Great gifts, no question, but more for him than for her and the sort of thing a man buys when he's left it too late. This should never happen, of course, because an alert husband will plan weeks and months in advance. He'll listen out for any subtle (or not so subtle) hints she may have dropped in the weeks leading up to her birthday and make a mental note. If need be, he'll write them down, because many husbands have the memory of a goldfish and forget everything they've been told within eight seco . . . erm . . . er . . . Sorry, what was the question?

Something of Sentimental Value

Often the amount of money you spend on a present is far less important than the thought or effort that went into choosing the gift. For example, put together an album of sentimental photos from when you first met or an old-fashioned mix-tape of her favourite songs from your early days together and you'll be marked very highly on both thought and originality. (You may lose points for making a tape and not a CD, of course, because nobody plays tapes any more, but she can't fault your effort.)

Expensive, Tasteful, Silky Underwear
In the Right Size

Don't go into a shop, stare blankly at the sales assistant and mime with your hands the approximate shape of your wife. If you don't know her size, do the simple thing and look at the labels in her underwear before you go out. Crucially, though, make sure she doesn't catch you poking around in her smalls. At worst she'll think you have unsavoury habits, at best she'll cotton on to your plan and scupper the big surprise. Oh, and note that it says 'tasteful' in the heading and bear in mind that you're buying the underwear for her, not you, which means any skimpy cheese-wire designs that you find particularly alluring are almost certainly out. Think sexy but classy, and opt for safe colours such as black or champagne.

The Latest Novel by Her Favourite Author – or a Book She Loved from Her Childhood

This shows you really have been listening to her, rather than just glazing over and nodding blankly, as so many failing husbands seem to do. Get this right and it will make you seem thoughtful and sensitive – which is never a bad thing. And going that extra mile and getting your hands on a first edition will make it even more special.

Personal Shopper

If you're one of the many men who watches his wife stagger into the department store's changing room, weighed down with more clothes than she can carry, only to finally re-emerge hot and bothered with nothing to show for it all, you have two options. Become an expert in women's fashion, which will show willing but take several years, or take the short cut and hire her a personal shopper. These professional stylists will know where to take your wife for the clothes best suited to her, and they will offer advice and solutions to any questions she has. Best of all, at no point will they look blank when asked for an opinion and request if they can go home yet.

A Pampering Weekend at a Health Spa

A weekend away being pampered? What's not to love about that? And given that you get to join her it's a win-win situation.

Jewellery

Always a very popular present, provided it's well chosen. Study her existing jewellery first and buy accordingly. For example, if she always wears simple silver pieces, don't buy chunky gold jewellery. And expect extra credit for buying matching sets – earrings and a necklace or bracelet – which show that you've put some thought into it. Earlier in this passage we said that the thought often counts for more than any fiscal outlay, and it's true enough. But where jewellery's concerned, you really do get what you pay for.

> *'The husband who wants a happy marriage should learn to keep his mouth shut and his chequebook open.'*
> **Groucho Marx**

Hotel Break

This is simple enough. You simply ask her to pack something for the weekend but don't let her know where you're going until you get there. Her excitement will be mounting with each mile, so choose wisely and don't spoil it all by pulling into the car park of a motel with a 'scenic' view of the motorway. To score higher still, make the hotel break in Paris, and head off on the Eurostar for a weekend in the undisputed capital of romance. If you're not both fluent French speakers, learn a few key phrases before you go to show that you've covered all the bases.

Journey Back in Time

Forget the grind of the daily commute and take a journey on one of the most magical trains in the world: the 08:49 First Transpennine Express from Cleethorpes to Briddlingt... ah, no, only joking. We refer, of course, to the world famous Orient Express. Step on board and you'll be whisked away to a bygone era, with armchairs, table lamps, white linen and immaculately dressed waiters. Dinner or lunch for two, departing from London's Victoria Station and taking a circular tour, is the perfect way to dine, and travel, in style.

Surprise, Surprise

Ultimately, only you can decide what is the perfect present to buy your wife, based on what you know she likes and dislikes. However, remember that buying your wife a present when it's not a special occasion and tapping into the element of surprise will count for even more (see p. 88 for some ideas). That's not to say you're free to forget her birthday if you buy her presents at other times of the year, of course. That would be a huge and terrible mistake, punishable by death.

The Art of Compromise

There will be times when you and your beloved don't agree, and it's good to learn sooner rather than later that it's best not to be an ass and shout each other down, but to try to listen to each other and allow a bit of give and take. To this end you are now provided with the rules of compromise:

♦ There are two sides to every argument. You may be convinced that you are right, but try putting yourself in her shoes and imagine why she is thinking in a different way to you. Perhaps you are both right – problems are rarely black and white.

♦ You are not expected to have all the answers and solutions. Sometimes just listening to your wife's problems or difficulties and showing some understanding is all she needs.

♦ Explain yourself. Don't expect her to be able to read your mind. If you are angry or upset about something she has done, then tell her how you feel in a calm and reasonable manner.

- Let her have her freedom and you can have your own.

- You are not the master of the household. A marriage consists of two equal partners. So don't try to control things. Discuss them between yourselves. Remember the old saying: 'A problem shared is a problem halved.'

- Don't be a stranger to housework, shopping or looking after the children. It should be a shared responsibility so embrace it like an old friend!

- Don't waste time sulking after an argument. It means so much more to say sorry for heated words – even if you know you were right!

- You may not want to do something that she wants to do or go where she does, such as go to the ballet or a romantic comedy, but do it with good grace. The alternative is a single life. And this book is for husbands.

Sorry, But . . .

Let's face it: nobody likes admitting they are wrong and having to apologize. It's far simpler just to make an excuse for your behaviour. And anyhow, you can't just go around telling the whole truth all the time. Whoever heard anyone say that they didn't do something because they were too lazy? Sometimes an excuse is the only way forward. Here are some that have been successfully tried and tested.

'I haven't washed up yet because I was waiting to make you a cup of tea and then do it all in one go.'

◆

'I did go for a quick drink after work but I was looking at some holiday brochures to find us somewhere nice to go.'

◆

'I know I forgot your birthday but, to me, you never seem to age.'

◆

'I didn't take the bin out because you can be fined for taking it out too early.'

◆

'I didn't wash the car because I thought there was still a hosepipe ban.'

◆

'It's not ecologically friendly to mow the lawn too often. Each time, thousands of microscopic wonders of wildlife are massacred.'

'I wasn't sick because of alcohol. I had a dodgy prawn that caused a stomach upset.'

◆

'Yes, there was a football game on TV but I was only watching it while the paint dried.'

◆

'I didn't fill the car up with fuel in case someone stole it overnight; that would have been a terrible waste of money.'

◆

'I was going to take the dog for a walk but he was so excited when I got the lead out that he ran round and round chasing his tail and exhausted himself before we got going.'

Surprise!

Everybody loves a surprise, provided it's a pleasant surprise and not one of those nasty hand-buzzers or squirty little plastic flowers. Nice surprises are, by their very nature, nice, and should be part of every husband's romantic arsenal. Used sparingly and timed just right, they can take a marriage to new heights.

Quite how – and with what – you choose to surprise your wife is entirely up to you and will be determined partly by the size of your bank balance but mainly by the size of your imagination. Far better to put more genuine thought into what you're surprising her with than to just throw your money away with little thought or imagination.

If you need inspiration, the following examples may help. But be warned, for further on in this chapter are several examples of how poor planning can scupper a surprise and turn cheers into tears.

Cheers

Exhibit A

For her birthday, Carl secretly bought his wife, Kristen, a painting that she had fallen in love with at a local art gallery. On the day itself he gave her all the other presents she had asked for and that evening they spent having dinner at their best friends' house. Unbeknownst to Kristen, however, Carl had arranged for the painting to be hung on the wall facing her at the dinner table. During the course of the dinner it took her a while before she noticed it, but when she did, her face was a picture of surprise and confusion. Kristen was startled that her friends had bought the painting, until Carl broke the news that it was hers to take home.

Exhibit B

Sarah had a wonderful surprise fortieth birthday when her husband, Nigel, took her on a mystery tour. He had told her to pack some clothes for a weekend away, including her best cocktail dress, but she had no idea where she was going. When they arrived at a vast and stunning country house, she couldn't believe that they were staying there. But she was in for another surprise when she entered and saw her best friends waiting to welcome her. Nigel then explained that they would all be getting dressed for dinner – men in dinner jackets, women in glamorous dresses – and sitting down for a banquet in the grand dining hall.

Exhibit C

Admittedly, not everyone can afford to pay Paul McCartney to play at a private birthday gig, but if your pockets are deep and you know the right people, it seems it can be possible. To celebrate TV producer Wendy Whitworth's fiftieth birthday in San Diego, California, Macca agreed to perform a special surprise set in front of 150 guests.

He didn't come cheap, of course, and Wendy's husband paid one million dollars to McCartney, which the star, who usually declines such requests, donated to charity.

'When Paul McCartney walked on stage I thought somebody was playing a trick on me,' said Wendy. 'It was so exciting: I couldn't believe it.'

The ninety-minute set – Sir Paul's first ever private concert – included the Beatles classics 'Yesterday', 'Hey Jude', 'Let It Be', 'Hello Goodbye' and 'I Saw Her Standing There'.

He then called Wendy on to the stage and presented her with fifty roses as the band broke into the Beatles track 'Birthday'. The lesson here, gentlemen: aim high.

The relationship between husband and wife should be one of closest friends.
B. R. Ambedkar

Some Surprising Ideas to
Get You Started

♦ Take your wife to a restaurant or bar where there is a pianist or a live band playing. Excuse yourself to go to the toilet and suddenly, appear on the stage to sing her favourite song, dedicated to her. If you can sing, that is. Otherwise this might not go down so well …

♦ Blindfold your wife and drive to a surprise destination. Offer tantalizing clues along the way but don't give out the secret until you arrive, whether it's a hotel, restaurant surprise gathering with friends, hot air balloon ride, or whatever creative idea you can come up with.

♦ Surprise your wife with dinner at a hotel restaurant, or meet in a hotel bar for a drink after work. When the bill arrives, casually tell the waiter to put it on your room tab. Then explain to your startled wife that you have booked a room for the night and that you've packed an overnight bag of clothes for her.

Tears

Sometimes no matter how hard you try, you just can't get it right – take these poor sods ...

Exhibit A

When a husband from Adelaide (who shall remain anonymous) came home from work early to surprise his wife on their wedding anniversary, he got a surprise of his own. His romantic plan had been to decorate the house with balloons and anniversary banners to surprise her when she came home from work and to cook her a romantic dinner. But after the excited hubby let himself into the house, he heard voices upstairs. Thinking there were intruders, he tip-toed his way up the stairs and entered the bedroom, armed with a heavy ornament. There in the marital bed he found his wife with another man. What happened next went unreported, sadly.

Exhibit B

Like many a romantic notion dreamed up in the pub, it seemed like such a good idea at the time. So after he left his local hostelry, Graeme Bethell decided it would be fun to pay his girlfriend a visit.

The only problem was that she lived on one side of the River Deben near Felixstowe in Suffolk, UK, and he was stood on the other. Going by road would take too long, but the rowing boat he spotted moored on the riverbank seemed the perfect solution. Unfortunately, the young Romeo wasn't put off by the fact that the boat had no oars, no engine and no sail, nor by the fact that he couldn't swim. He just imagined that the boat would gently glide across to the opposite shore. Only it didn't, and instead drifted out to sea on the tide and left our hapless hero clinging to the craft and praying that he wouldn't be run down by passing ships.

The alarm was eventually raised the following morning when a walker on the beach saw his struggles and a fishing boat towed him back to shore. 'It was meant to be a bit of a romantic surprise to turn up and see her in a boat,' he said. 'Instead, it ended up becoming the most terrifying experience of my life.'

Notorious Husbands

Some men just don't make husband material ...

Rod Stewart

He famously asked 'Do Ya Think I'm Sexy?' in one of his hit songs and, it seems, many women do.

In 1979, Rod got married for the first time, to George Hamilton's ex-wife, Alana, with whom he had two children. Following their divorce, he had a child with model Kelly Emberg and then tied the knot with Australian supermodel Rachel Hunter in 1990, fathering two more kids before yet another divorce. He completed the hat-trick in 2007 when he said 'I do' to photographer Penny Lancaster. They have one child. But it's not just a case of a pretty face with Rod. Oh, no. They need to be blonde and leggy, too.

In reference to his many failed relationships and what they had cost him financially, he was once quoted as saying, 'Instead of getting married again, I'm going to find a woman I don't like and just give her a house.'

Ashley Cole

The England footballer allegedly scored away from home with 22-year-old hairdresser Aimee Walton in December 2007. His wife, Girls Aloud singer Cheryl – one of the prettiest women in pop – was sick as a parrot when she found out.

A contrite Ashley apparently grovelled that he was drunk,

that it was a one-night stand and a huge mistake, etc etc – but just when it looked as if he was about to be substituted, Cheryl had a change of heart. She gave him another chance to show that he could be good both on and off the pitch, which just goes to show that marriage is a game of two halves and that it's not over until the final whistle.

King Henry VIII

Any new bride naturally feels jittery on her wedding day, but particularly if she happens to be marrying King Henry VIII ...

In 1509 Henry married Catherine of Aragon, but divorced her in 1533 after falling in love with Anne Boleyn, who had recently come to his court. When he grew bored of Anne, he didn't bother going through a messy divorce again – he simply had her beheaded in 1536. Shortly afterwards, he married his third wife, Jane Seymour, but she died later that year.

Determined to make a good marriage fourth time round, Henry agreed to wed German princess Anne of Cleves without having met her. When she arrived in England, he is said to have found her rude and ugly. He went through with the wedding nonetheless, but it ended in divorce after six months. He went on to marry the young and pretty Catherine Howard in 1540, but flew into a jealous rage when he discovered that she had previously been engaged to another man – and possibly a second. Henry ordered both men and his wife to be beheaded. By 1543, he was fat and ill and his new wife, Catherine Parr, was as much his nurse as his wife. They remained married until he died in 1547 – a lucky escape for her and no mistake!

Mickey Rooney

The veteran Hollywood actor married seven times before seeming to have found Mrs Right. Here's the run-down: Ava Gardner (1942–43, divorced); Betty Jane Rase (1944–49, divorced); Martha Vickers (1949–51, divorced); Elaine Mahnken (1952–58, divorced); Barbara Ann Thomason (1958–66, died); Margie Lane (1966–67, divorced); Carolyn Hockett (1969–74, divorced) and Jan Chamberlin (1978–present).

When asked why it took him seven marriages before Jan to settle down once and for all, Mickey replied, 'My partners weren't what we call, in horse-racing parlance, routers. They were sprinters. They went out of the gate, but then they stopped. They couldn't go the distance.' Hmm … Comparing your ex-wives to horses, Mickey? We're beginning to get the picture.

Bill Clinton

The former US president famously declared, 'I did not have sexual relations with that woman.' Well, that was not quite how everyone else interpreted his goings-on in the Oval Office with Monica Lewinsky.

In 1995, twenty-one-year-old Monica Lewinsky was hired as a White House intern and was immediately struck by the president's charisma. She loved working close to Clinton and he, too, seemed to grow equally enamoured. Monica later claimed she had had nine sexual encounters with him in his private office, in a hallway, and even once when he was on the phone. After her good 'friend' Linda Tripp secretly recorded her phone conversations with Monica, these claims soon became very public knowledge.

Clinton, with his wife Hillary standing by her man, declared the allegations to be false (at one point resorting to the argument 'it depends on what the meaning of the word "is" is'), but when Monica produced her now-infamous stained blue dress, Clinton was forced to admit that he had indeed had an 'improper physical relationship' with her.

Nero

The phrase 'power-mad' certainly summed up Roman Emperor Nero, who came to power in 54 AD, at the age of sixteen.

Dissatisfied with his marriage to Octavia, he began an affair with Claudia Acte, a former slave. He then became romantically involved with Poppaea Sabina, the wife of his friend (and future emperor) Otho. Nero's mother, Agrippina, wasn't best pleased with her son's wayward behaviour and sided with his put-upon wife, prompting Nero to have his mother assassinated and his wife banished and later executed. He was thus free to marry the pregnant Poppaea, but their wedded bliss came to an abrupt end when he kicked her to death when she complained that he'd come home late from the races.

Nero was also known to be a lover of young boys, and he 'married' two men in succession, both in public ceremonies involving all the ritual appropriate to legal marriage. He had a pretty young slave boy, Sporus, castrated and then went through a public wedding ceremony to make the boy his 'wife'. Later, reversing roles and dispensing with the castration, Nero made a chap called Doryphorus marry him, making the young man his 'husband'.

George Clooney

Chisel-jawed Hollywood ladies' man George Clooney isn't like the other men on this list because, rather than being the type of cad who says 'I do' before running off with the first willing filly to give him the eye, gorgeous George has hit upon a foolproof way of guaranteeing he never cheats on his wife. He simply never marries her in the first place.

He's vehemently anti-marriage, you see, and apparently doesn't think a piece of paper telling you you're married makes much sense. It wasn't always thus. Back in 1989 he tied the knot with actress Talia Balsam, but that lasted just four years before they went their separate ways – she off to obscurity, he to find fame and untold fortune.

Nowadays, the star of *Oceans 11*, *Oceans 12*, *Oceans etc.* can have his pick of the world's most agreeable ladies, but none are likely to be walking down the aisle with him any time soon. Particularly as it was reported in the *National Enquirer* that George has erected a strange anti-marriage memorial in one of his homes in the form of his old wedding ring strung on a ribbon with the ends tied to two candlesticks. 'It's not like he has anything against the institution of marriage,' said the 'friend' quoted in the piece, 'it's just not for him. As far as tying the knot again, George has said "Been there, done that, won't do it again." That's how he's explained his wedding ring memorial.'

Confirmation, perhaps, that George Clooney is blessed with far more money than sense.

A Wedding Anniversary to Remember

The first wedding anniversary tends to be the most exciting, and the one most couples make the biggest fuss over. With the wedding still a relatively recent event, there's plenty of scope for saying 'Gosh, doesn't time fly?' – and a good chance that you will both remember the date!

One novel way of celebrating an anniversary, and particularly the first, is to recreate aspects of your Big Day. Decorate a room in the same way as for your wedding reception, with flowers, ribbons and so on, and then share a romantic meal right in the middle of it, on a table with a linen tablecloth and napkins – and, of course, plenty of bubbly.

If it's not too fiddly, you could bake (or buy) a smaller version of your wedding cake, and then later on watch your wedding video and recreate your first dance.

However, if that doesn't appeal you could try one of the following:

♦ Spend a romantic night under the stars sleeping in a tent in your garden. Take a torch, snack and a bottle of wine and cuddle up to keep warm.

♦ Re-visit somewhere that you went to on an early date, whether it was a restaurant, bar, art gallery or park etc

♦ Enjoy a weekend away at a hotel in a room with a sea view or take in a romantic film at the cinema.

Getting It Right

Horace and Margaret Bunn had a date with royalty for their sixtieth wedding anniversary. The couple from Northumberland were guests of the Queen and Prince Philip, as they celebrated their own diamond wedding at Westminster Abbey at a high profile service in front of the nation.

They were one of a handful of couples traced by Buckingham Place, and invited to share the same wedding anniversary celebrations as the royal couple.

'It was an amazing day filled with amazing experiences,' said Horace. But it would never have happened if he had not taken the advice of his own father, sixty years ago.

'We were going to get married two days after the royal

wedding on 20 November, 1947,' he said. 'But my dad persuaded us to change the arrangements so that we were married on the same day as Princess Elizabeth, as she was then, and the Duke.

'After what happened to us we are glad we did. The whole experience, including shaking hands with the Queen and Duke, was just unforgettable and one we would never have dreamed about all those years ago when we married.'

Getting It wrong

Football fan Alan Holmes, from Fife, has travelled the length and breadth of Scotland visiting every football ground to have his picture taken outside. And he didn't let his wedding anniversary get in his way. Alan, who wore his beloved Raith Rovers strip in every photograph, dragged his long-suffering wife Caroline with him!

'It was our fourth wedding anniversary when I wanted to go north to Inverness, so I booked us a nice hotel and told her we were going away for the weekend,' he said. 'It was really romantic and she never realized that I had another motive until it was too late.

'We managed to see Inverness, Ross County and Elgin, although Caroline fell asleep midway.'

Just Plain Odd ...

Les Lailey celebrated his golden wedding anniversary by eating tinned chicken that was fifty years old! It was given to him as part of a hamper for a wedding present in 1956.

'We packed it away and kept it safe,' said Les, from Greater Manchester, England. 'I always said that I would eat it on my fiftieth wedding anniversary, so I did. It went down a treat. It smelt good and tasted all right – I didn't even bother heating it up.

'The family all rang the next day to ask if I was okay. I think they were expecting me to come down with something, but I was fine.'

The Wedding Anniversary
You Forgot

Unless you're the woman in this marriage (and we're guessing you're not), then your chances of somehow forgetting your wedding anniversary are depressingly high.

It's not necessarily your fault, of course, because men's brains are not programmed like women's. So while we have total recall on key fixtures for the coming football season and every Grand National winner since 1968, we can't retain the truly important dates for more than five minutes.

And that can be a problem, because if there's one thing guaranteed to break your good lady's heart clean in two, it's the belief that you don't care enough to remember the date you both walked down the aisle. (Or her birthday, knowing you.)

As a loving, caring and considerate husband, it is your job to remember the date and *never* ever forget it. Have it tattooed on the palm of your hand if you have to, but just make sure you never forget your anniversary, otherwise it's your balls on the block, and rightly so.

But what if somehow you do forget? What then? Well, you're a bloody fool and your only hope is to (a) think clearly and (b) put into practice the following Emergency Action Plan.

Emergency Action Plan

So, it's first thing in the morning, and your wife gives you a kiss. Nothing unusual there, only she follows it up with a card. It's not your birthday, is it? No, you know that much. In which case it must be . . . oh dear Lord, an anniversary card! Your blood runs cold. How could you have forgotten? The vital thing is to keep your head at this stage, and do not betray any signs of inner turmoil and rising panic.

Smile and attempt to look relaxed as you return her kiss and declare, 'Happy anniversary, darling.' Then say that you have planned a special treat for her of breakfast in bed. This buys you some time and the casual placement of the word 'planned' makes it look as if you are in control of the situation.

Now, as you are busy scrambling around in the kitchen desperately looking for something more appetizing for her to eat than a piece of toast, take the opportunity to turn this to your advantage. A quick shout up the stairs of, 'I'm just popping out to get some more eggs/orange juice/whatever,' will buy you all the time you need to completely take control of the situation.

From here on, it's plain sailing. In the car, down to the shops and buy the necessaries – card, flowers, chocolates. If you can get a bottle of champagne without the man behind the counter accusing you of being a raging drunk, then all the better, for you can then serve her a glass of bubbly with her breakfast or mix it with some orange juice, if she prefers. So, that's sorted then. But don't forget to get breakfast ingredients too, otherwise you will have to go back out again and she will definitely cotton on.

Quick fixes

Not everything always goes according to plan, of course, especially when there wasn't much of a plan to begin with. So here's some quick yet imaginative ideas that you can mix and match to save the day/your bacon.

Rock Solid

One part inspiration, one part perspiration, this: head to the garden outside your bedroom window and find as many large stones or rocks as it takes to spell 'I Love You' out in big letters on the front lawn. Make sure your wife pulls back the curtains for the gesture to have the impact it requires.

Radio Romance

If you're quick and you explain the sorry hole you find yourself in, it may be possible to call up a radio station to put in a last-minute anniversary request – with the obligatory soppy message.

Try the local stations rather than nationals, as they're more likely to indulge you, plus request a song you both like from when you first got together for added effect. If it's too late for a request, download the song instead and play it over breakfast.

Food For Thought

Speaking of breakfast, little touches at this stage could make all the difference. With as much artistic élan as you can muster, scrape a heart and her initials into the toast.

Modern Romance

If you're a thoroughly modern pair and both fully paid-up members of one of these new-fangled social networking sites, leave a slushy message on your site of choice declaring your undying love for your wife for all the world to see.

Love Poems

If you're modern enough to have internet access but not so advanced that you know what a social networking site might be, download some classic romantic poetry from the World Wide Web and have a poetry recital evening over a glass of wine. There are plenty of ones around to tug at the heartstrings. Overleaf are are some examples . . .

Love by Samuel Taylor Coleridge – 'All thoughts, all thoughts, all passions, all delights,/Whatever stirs this mortal frame,/Are all but ministers of Love,/And feed his sacred flame.'

The Sun Rising by John Donne – 'She's all states, and all princes I;/Nothing else is;/ Princes do but play us; compared to this,/All honour's mimic, all wealth alchemy.'

She Walks In Beauty Like the Night by Lord Byron – 'She walks in beauty like the night/Of cloudless climes and starry skies/And all that's best of dark and bright/Meets in her aspect and her eyes . . .'

Sonnet XVII by Pablo Neruda: 'I love you without knowing how, or when, or from where,/I love you simply, without problems or pride ...'

Traditional Anniversary Symbols

The tradition of giving a specific gift for each anniversary dates back to the Middle Ages. There are some variations in different countries but a good way around this is to combine these and add a modern twist. Here are some imaginative gift ideas that will make it look as if you have put in a lot of thought!

1st: Paper
Buy a scrapbook and stick in anything paper-based from your shared life together, such as theatre or cinema tickets, train tickets, photographs, holiday reservation forms and maps. Or book some tickets and present her with those.

2nd: Cotton
A visit to the world-famous Cotton Club in New York, where such legends as Duke Ellington, Count Basie, Cab Calloway, Ella Fitzgerald, Louis Armstrong and Billie Holiday have performed.

3rd: Leather
Saddle up and go horse-riding together.

4th: Fruit or flowers
(linen or silk in some countries)
Try a combination of dining out at a posh restaurant with white linen tablecloths, presenting her with flowers and having some fruit for dessert! As for the silk, that's up to you …

5th: Wood

An ornately carved Welsh love spoon – traditionally made by young men as a love token for their sweethearts.

6th: Sugar or iron

A trip to Paris to visit the Eiffel Tower, and some luxury Belgian chocolates to eat while you are up there enjoying the view!

7th: Wool or copper

A cashmere top or woollen coat that she can wear for a trip to London to have a photo taken next to a 'copper' (policeman).

8th: Bronze

Sun tan lotion in preparation for a bronzed body from a tropical dream holiday.

9th: Pottery

A visit to 'The Potteries', more officially named Stoke-on-Trent in Staffordshire, England. It's the world's largest and most famous pottery-producing city, where the great manufacturers such as Wedgwood, Doulton, Spode and Portmerion set up business. Visit the museums and watch the potters at work. Or join a pottery class so that you can recreate the famous potter's wheel scene from the movie *Ghost*!

10th: Tin

Fill a pretty tin with her favourite pampering products, sweets or jewellery.

15th: Crystal

Flute glasses and some Cristal champagne.

20th: China

Book a table for two at a Chinese restaurant or drink tea at the Ritz out of fine bone china cups.

30th: Pearl

An oyster dinner, of course (don't forget it's an aphrodisiac!).

40th: Ruby

A dozen ruby-red roses and a case of vintage red wine.

50th: Gold

Head for San Francisco and drive across the stunning Golden Gate Bridge.

60th: Diamond

A stay in the 'City of Diamonds' – Amsterdam. Visit the diamond museum and watch the process of cutting and polishing these beautiful gems at the Amsterdam Diamond Center.

70th: Platinum

The Platinum News is an online news site for the sun-kissed Virgin Islands. But why not go there and experience the real thing for yourselves!

80th: Oak

This is certainly one to celebrate! Barrels in which red wines, sherry, brandy and whisky are matured, are made from oak. It's time to party!

Becoming a Father

No one expects you to be an expert father the minute your wife
gives birth. Like all new dads, you will learn as you go along. If
you feel shocked, panicked or overwhelmed, remember you are
not alone. It's a huge step. But while your life will never be the
same again, the good news is that fatherhood brings its own
rewards.

10 Good Reasons to be a Dad

1 If it's a boy you can play with his toys.

2 If it's a girl, you'll think she is the prettiest daughter in the world.

3 For the first time you will appreciate what your own parents did for you.

4 Those kids you never noticed on the trains and in shops? Now, you'll find yourself smiling at them.

5 You can watch all those kids' movies you never got to see the first time round.

6 Experience again the childhood joy of playing and using your imagination.

7 Unconditional kisses and cuddles from your kids are priceless.

8 Watching them develop – walking, talking, gaining a character and a sense of humour – is fascinating.

9 You get an excuse to go on theme park rides.

10 They can repay you by looking after you in your dotage.

Before the Baby Arrives

Go to prenatal classes with your wife so that, as well as offering her support and taking an interest, you can get some idea of what to expect. Get the nursery decorated and choose a cot and baby clothes. Having a baby is one of life's great experiences so relish every moment.

During Birth

Your wife might scream and call you all sorts of names. The likelihood is she will have spent hours in labour prior to the birth, and, in case you weren't listening in prenatal classes, the whole process is exhausting and painful for her, so don't move from her side!

> 'When I was a boy of fourteen, my father was so ignorant I could hardly stand to have the old man around. But when I got to be twenty-one, I was astonished at how much the old man had learned in seven years.'
> **Mark Twain**

After the Baby Arrives

Yes, it is a shock to suddenly have this helpless bundle to care for. And if you weren't particularly the responsible type before, then you had better learn fast! Your wife's attentions will be focused fully on the baby for some time and you have to get used to it and help her out as much as possible. That's what fathers are for.

For the first few weeks or months, you may not get much sleep during the night because the baby will cry and demand feeding, but this stage won't last forever. And anyway, it's remarkable how you adjust to it and are still able to function the following day despite sleep derivation.
You can always blame your kids for …

▶ The mess that you made.
▶ Being late anywhere.
▶ Needing to get home from a boring party/dinner/family gathering.
▶ Having played with something you can't find.
▶ Needing so much attention that you were unable to do the housework whilst your wife was out.

Heroic Husbands

There's not much call for the traditional knight in shining armour these days, but that doesn't mean you can shirk your responsibilities: an act of bravery (or just complete unselfishness) will transform you into a truly heroic husband.

Real-Life Crocodile Dundee

Saving your wife from the jaws of a crocodile rates pretty highly on the heroic deeds scale. In April 2008, Norm Pethrick did just that when he leapt onto the back of an eight-foot crocodile that had seized his wife from a riverbank at Litchfield National Park, Australia.

Wendy had been crouching on the bank washing her face when the crocodile lunged, locking its jaws on both of her thighs and dragging her into the water. Norm jumped on the reptile and poked its eyes until it released her. 'I just jumped on top of it,' he told reporters from his hospital bed. 'There's no time for fear, you see, when you want to save someone, especially someone you love.'

Mrs Pethrick suffered serious bite wounds to her legs as she tried to prise the crocodile's jaws apart, but the general manager of the Royal Darwin Hospital said that she was saved by her husband's 'swift and diligent actions'.

The Ultimate Valentine's Day Gift

On Valentine's Day 2008, Carolyn Coburn received more than a bouquet of flowers from her husband Bruce. He gave her half of his liver – an act of love that saved her life.

The couple, from Michigan, USA, had been married for twelve years. In 2005, Carolyn had been diagnosed with a rare genetic disease called auto-immune hepatitis, and later learnt she'd have to be put on a liver transplant list. Fearing that the list was too long, Bruce asked if his liver would be compatible. When tests showed that it was, he immediately offered to make the donation. 'I wanted to avoid having her on a list,' he said. 'The disease would only get worse. It was a no-brainer for me.'

Initially, Carolyn said that she and the hospital surgeon, Dr Atsushi Yoshida, were against the living donation from Bruce because of their three children. 'We could both have died during surgery,' she said. 'I didn't want our kids left without parents.'

But the operation eventually went ahead and proved successful. 'It's a very amazing thing for me,' said Carolyn. 'That he has that much love for me … to risk his own life, so I can watch my kids grow up.'

Dr Yoshida was so moved that he came over all poetic: 'They gave each other their hearts when they first got married. Now they share a liver.'

Gallant Groom

Michael and Joanne Noone's wedding meal had just finished, and the newly married couple were looking forward to the evening's entertainment at their reception in a hotel in Co. Kildare, Ireland.

But as they were waiting for the band to set up, the suspended ceiling collapsed on the gathering and 130 guests were lucky to escape with their lives.

The brave groom flung himself over his new wife in a bid to protect her from the shower of steel and plaster. Guests ran from the room in terror and fourteen of the injured were rushed to hospital.

Michael was hailed a hero for protecting his wife and helping get shocked guests out of the building. 'I just ran to the wall with Joanne and I got her down on the ground,' he said. 'It was terrifying to see a ceiling coming in.'

A Good Rollicking

A wife who fell into a coma after losing her baby during a difficult labour came back from the brink of death after her husband lost his temper with her.

Yvonne Sullivan, from Weston-super-Mare, Somerset, contracted severe blood poisoning and lost consciousness. Her husband, Dominic, kept a round-the-clock vigil at her bedside for two weeks as she lay in intensive care. But when doctors told him they might have to switch off her life support machine, Dominic got angry and gave his wife a firm telling-off.

Dominic left the room to get some fresh air and returned two hours later to find Yvonne had started to breathe. Within five days doctors were able to switch off her ventilator. When she regained consciousness, she saw her husband standing beside her. She remembered hearing her husband yelling at her as she lay in a coma and said it gave her the strength to pull through.

'I can't remember exactly what he said but I never like getting told off by Dom,' she said. 'Something inside me just clicked and I began to fight again. When I came round, I thought he'd been gone a few minutes; then he told me I'd been out for two weeks. It's a miracle. I owe him so much.'

A Mucky Story

Ryan Severn made the ultimate rescue attempt when his wife's wedding ring rolled down a drain. He went down into the sewer to find it!

The pair, from Seattle, USA, made extra cash by cleaning offices at the weekend and it was on one such occasion that Ryan's wife Ann removed her wedding ring so that it wouldn't get tarnished while she was scrubbing.

'She took off the ring and it was like watching a movie as it started rolling toward the drain,' said Ryan. He lunged for the ring but it was gathering speed and the pair watched in horror as it disappeared through the grate.

'Ann started crying and I said, "You know what? I've got a plan."' The devoted hubby bought a wetsuit and built a makeshift strainer, then climbed down into the drain in the middle of the night. But after sifting through the muck, he came up empty-handed. 'It was disgusting and stinky and I was really disheartened not to have found it,' he said.

Eventually he called in the professionals to pump out the water and the ring was uncovered, cleaned thoroughly and put back on Ann's finger, where it belonged.

The Art of Interpretation

People don't always mean what they say, but when you're married you need to be able to interpret what is really going on in each other's heads. Don't make the mistake of being too literal in your thinking – try to work out the hidden meaning of loaded comments. The most frequently used phrases and questions have helpfully been decoded for you below.

'Do you know what day it is?'
(For goodness' sake, don't say 'Wednesday' – it's your anniversary.)

'I'll do it.'
(You do it.)

'I'm fine.'
(I'm not.)

'You need a break. You've been working too hard.'
(I need a break. Book us a holiday.)

'I suppose I had better tidy the house.'
(Why don't you do some housework?)

'I've no idea what to cook tonight.'
(Let's go to a restaurant.)

'You do whatever you want to do.'
(Just you wait. It's my turn next.)

> *'By all means marry. If you get a good wife you will become happy, and if you get a bad one you will become a philosopher.'*
> **Socrates**

Keeping the Marriage Alive

After you have been married for a while, it is easy to become complacent and take your wife for granted. So it's important to take the time every now and then to ask yourself what attracted you to her – and vice versa – in the first place. Are you still the man your wife married? She may once have considered you fun, exciting and spontaneous, but that doesn't mean she still does. You have to work at keeping a marriage alive; here's a guide to doing it right.

> *'You know something, folks, as ridiculous as this sounds, I would rather feel the sweet breath of my beautiful wife on the back of my neck as I sleep, than stuff dollar bills into some stranger's G-string.'*
> **Homer Simpson**

Talk, Listen, Learn

Sounds easy, doesn't it? But how often do you really take the time to sit down and talk to each other? Just take a break – whether it's over dinner at home, a lunchtime drink or in a restaurant – it's important to discuss your feelings and to talk about your job, and your hopes and fears. But don't hog the conversation: make sure you listen to what your wife has to say. Whatever it is that's on your mind, it's good to share things. Remember, you are a team.

Movie Magic

Recreate those exciting dating movies of your youth by bringing the magic of the silver screen into your home. Snuggle up on the settee, dim the lights and wallow in a slushy DVD. Here are some of the most romantic movies of all time:

Only You
City of Angels
On Golden Pond
An Affair to Remember
Ghost
Roman Holiday
Love Actually
The African Queen
Titanic
Four Weddings
  and a Funeral

Dr Zhivago
Sleepless in Seattle
Barefoot in the Park
Don Juan DeMarco
When Harry Met Sally
Notting Hill
Il Postino
Casablanca
Love Story
The Bridges of Madison
  County

Charm Offensive

Take a tip from your wife's fantasy men. Who does she like in the public eye? We can't all be Sean Connery, Johnny Depp or David Beckham, but dig a little deeper because, with a bit of luck, there might be more to their attraction other than looks, fame, fortune and talent!

Connery is noted for his charm and good humour, for example – well, that's not beyond the rest of us. Depp is modest and sensitive – if it doesn't come naturally then work on it. And Beckham has that dazzling smile – well, you could try cheering up a bit! The thing is to make the most of your attributes. You probably did in the beginning but it might be time to start using them again.

When was the last time you said 'I love you'? Or spontaneously kissed or cuddled her or held her hand? It's these little things, not the grand gesture, that matter the most.

You Gotta Laugh

Just the physical act of laughing makes us feel better. But when was the last time you laughed along with your wife? Jokes, amusing anecdotes and a quick wit put the pep back into relationships and help us to cope with the pressures of life.

Do something foolish or frivolous. Perhaps something that made you both laugh in the past. Have fun at a roller-skating rink, enjoy a snowball fight or even a spontaneous pillow fight. Go and watch your favourite comedian perform or have a day at the seaside and an amusement arcade. These are some simple pleasures that can have a big impact in your life.

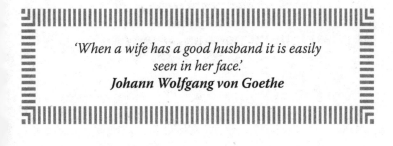

'When a wife has a good husband it is easily seen in her face.'
Johann Wolfgang von Goethe

Personal Appearance

Just because you are married, it doesn't mean that you no longer have to think about your appearance. The decomposition from dashing man about town to couch potato is such a slow process that it can happen without you realizing it.

The unshaven, slipper-clad, food-stained tracksuit-bottoms look is not attractive. You wouldn't find it attractive in a woman, after all, so what makes you think that you can get away with it?

Think Cary Grant, Hugh Grant (anyone Grant, probably – except Russell). Forget Jim Royle and Johnny Vegas and put in a bit of an effort.

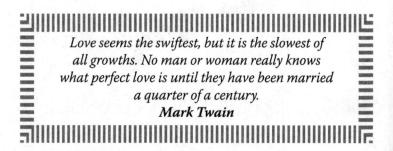

Love seems the swiftest, but it is the slowest of all growths. No man or woman really knows what perfect love is until they have been married a quarter of a century.
Mark Twain

Empty Nest

Do you remember those days before you had kids? When you had freedom to do what you liked, when you liked, without having to worry whether you were being selfish?

The odd thing is that, although they often pine for those days, parents don't quite know what to do with themselves once they get them back. We're talking 'Empty Nest Syndrome' here. The kids have grown up and gone and the pair of you have the house to yourselves for the first time in twenty-odd years. But while being a couple rather than a full-time family worked fine in the early years, suddenly it all seems rather quiet and lonely.

Okay, you are older and perhaps less inclined to stay out raving until the early hours, but it's important to grasp the opportunity to do all the things that you didn't have much time to do while the kids were at home. Enjoy the peace inside the house – and when it seems too quiet, go out!

Is This Our House?

Things will certainly look different around the house, but your concerns may well disappear when you realize that:

- ▶ The house stays clean
- ▶ There are no smelly socks in the bedroom, on the landing,
  all down the stairs, etc.
- ▶ There's food in the fridge
- ▶ The grocery bills are lower
- ▶ There's no loud music thumping through the house
- ▶ There's no queue for the bathroom
- ▶ The 'taxi' has reverted to being your car
- ▶ The phone bill is drastically cheaper
- ▶ The TV actually has a remote control – and you are in charge of it
- ▶ You can be passionate with your wife without being interrupted – even in the front room!

Rekindling the Romance

This is a new chapter in your life and a wonderful chance to kick-start your relationship. For a long time, much of your attention and energy will have been directed towards your children. Now you can refocus on yourselves. Visualize those happy and carefree days before you became parents, and try to recapture that mood.

Free From the Shackles!

Without kids to feed, you can enjoy eating and drinking out more often, meeting friends and socializing. What about a weekly trip to the cinema? You will have more time to indulge in your favourite hobbies, or find new ones. Make a list of things you have never done but would like to do, or places you would like to visit. Whatever you do, make sure you do something rather than sitting in silence in front of the telly, like a couple of miserable bookends!

Rooms To Fill

What a lovely problem to have! For years you will have been complaining about the mess and not having enough space to put everything in. Now you have empty bedrooms to do what you like with. Well ... they should be empty, but kids have a tendency to leave behind all the clutter that they don't want in their new homes. So give them an ultimatum. Tell them to take it with them or threaten to throw it away.

Okay, so if they are the type of children who visit often and stay over, it's politic to leave their beds *in situ*. Otherwise, come up with a plan for the room that means both of you will want to use it: a spare study perhaps, or an extra lounge so that if one of you is watching something on TV that the other one doesn't want to see, you can go and watch it in the new room.

Of course, if there really are too many rooms for the pair of you, then you could consider down-sizing and frittering away the profit on all kinds of indulgences: holidays, a cruise, a new car …

Congratulate Yourself

You can feel satisfied and even a tad smug. The job of being a parent is never done, but you have achieved the main thing: raising a child to become a respectable, well-rounded, independent young adult. So give each other a pat on the back!

Silence is Golden

Things You Should Never Say to Your Wife

Sometimes you just can't help putting your foot in it, but over the years you come to realize that often it is wiser to keep your mouth shut than risk making some clangers such as the ones below:

▶ 'My ex-wife/ex-girlfriend had a good way of doing that.'

▶ 'I preferred your hair the way it was.'

▶ 'Sorry, I wasn't listening.'

▶ 'You sound just like your mother.'

▶ 'Does that dress still fit you?'

▶ 'Can you sort out the kids, please?'

Screen Husbands

Tell No One (2007)

This French film of the Harlan Coben thriller provides all husbands with a role model in the character of Alex Beck. When his beloved wife is seemingly murdered, Alex cannot get over her – and eight years on is still devoted to her memory when he receives an email from her, with the subject heading, 'Tell no one'. He sets out on a terrifying journey to find out whether·or not his wife is still alive. As well as being a rip-roaring thriller, *Tell No One* really does demonstrate the meaning of eternal love.

What Happens in Vegas (2008)

Ashton Kutcher and Cameron Diaz as Jack and Joy show how marriage shouldn't be done – i.e. getting married whilst severely intoxicated in Vegas. Although they decide to go their separate ways, after he wins $3,000,000 on a slot machine she claims half since they are legally wed. The case goes to court and a judge deems that they have to live together for six months to attempt to make the marriage work. So Joy moves in with Jack and both try to drive each other to divorce since whoever leaves will not keep the money. But perhaps the sloshed shotgun-style wedding isn't such a bad idea after all – as little by little they start to fall for each other ... (Before attempting to replicate this scenario, just remember Britney and Jason. Jason who? Precisely.)

La Vita è Bella (1997)

A real weepy this one. It's an unlikely sounding romantic comedy since it's set in a concentration camp. A father, played by Roberto Benigni, entertains his son in the camp. The boy's mother is at the same camp, but along with all the other women is separated from the male prisoners; in a poignantly romantic scene Benigni plays some music through the window to let her know he is thinking of her. Just shows you don't always have to say it with words.

You, Me and Dupree (2006)

This movie starring Kate Hudson and Matt Dillon as newlyweds takes a funny look at the difficulties faced by the couple when their best man, Dupree, moves in with them after he loses his job. Unfortunately he proceeds to treat their house as his own home, bringing with him his stuffed moose head, and sleeping naked on their couch. An extreme example of how friendships have to change once you get married!

Shrek (2001, 2004, 2007)

In this series of three animated films (a fourth is in production) a faithful and courageous ogre falls in love with a beautiful princess who coincidentally turns out to be an ogre; marries her; rescues her from numerous situations; fights off evil forces and embraces married life and fatherhood. Living proof that good looks doesn't necessarily always win the fair princess (even if she does turn into green ogre ...).

Mr & Mrs Smith (2005)

Marriage Counselor:	On a scale of one to ten, how would you rate the happiness of your marriage?
Jane Smith:	Eight.
John Smith:	Wait. Could you clarify? Is ten the highest? Ten being perfectly happy and one being totally miserable or . . .
Marriage Counselor:	Just respond instinctively.
John Smith:	Ok. Ready?
Jane Smith, John Smith:	Eight.

Mad Men (2008)

Now a quick look to TV for a good example of how not to behave as a husband – hit show *Mad Men*'s Don Draper, the seemingly perfect advertising executive, appears to have it all: he's dashingly good looking, talented, successful, and married to the very beautiful Elizabeth ('Betty'), yet he nevertheless manages to still be unsatisfied, and embarks on a series of affairs. Learn to appreciate what you've got, gentlemen.

The Simpsons (1989-present)

And finally – star of television and film – Mr Homer Simpson. Yes, he's a slob, addicted to doughnuts, and his abilities as a good father are questionable, but no one can fault Homer for his utter devotion to his wife and children. He even divorces Marge so they can get married a second time since their first wedding wasn't the magical one she had dreamed of. Which just goes to show that you don't have to be a great man to be a great husband.

Which Husband Are You?

Husbands come in many different shapes, sizes and styles; from the ultra-macho Alpha Male to the thumb-sucking Mummy's Boy. Not sure which one you might be? Then read on . . .

The Alpha Male

This man still thinks of himself as a hunter-gatherer. He considers his wife helpless without him. He's loud and competitive and would list his 'likes' as sport, winning, driving fast and using power tools. Beneath the tough exterior there is a heart, but he rarely shows it, because emotion is for girls and wimps.

    Most likely to say: 'Leave it to me, sweetheart.'
    Will never say: 'Actually, you're right. You know best.'

The Puppy

Ever eager to please, he'll do just about anything to earn his wife's praise. Takes his orders to 'go fetch' like a faithful hound, and why would she want a lapdog when she has a husband like this at her beck and call? His attentive and obedient nature is admirable in many ways, but maddening in others.

    Most likely to say: 'Put your feet up: I'll make you a cup of tea.'
    Will never say: 'What's for dinner, then?'

The Iron Man

He's never happier than when covered in mud and undertaking his next test of endurance and manliness. He'll spend most weekends away running marathons in every city in the world (he's nearly done them all) and his idea of a romantic summer getaway is climbing Everest or swimming the Amazon. His wife had better be made of stern stuff to keep up with him, or resign herself to cheering him on from the sidelines of the World Log-Tossing/Ice-Wrestling/Ultimate Fighting Championships.

Most likely to say: "I need to stock up on energy bars."
Will never say: 'It's a bit cold for a walk – let's snuggle up and watch *The Antiques Roadshow*.'

The Career Guy

A natural born provider, the career guy is married to the job as much as to his poor wife, and if he can't be in the office then he's talking about it. He's not interested in how his wife's day has been; that's just not important. Certainly not as important as his job, which is really very important indeed. So important in fact that he starts work the second he gets on the train and can often be overheard by the whole carriage blabbing loudly into his mobile about some important business or other.

Most likely to say: 'No time for that; I've got important calls to make.'

Will never say: 'So how was your day, darling?'

The Bore

At any social gathering this husband will attempt to 'trump' any story with a more interesting anecdote of his own – but he fails time after time after time. Incredibly, he doesn't realize this and continues to be a one-man conversation stopper. You can't help but feel sorry for his embarassed wife, although she did marry him so maybe not.

Most likely to say: 'Ha, that's *nothing . . .*'
Will never say: 'Wow! That's really interesting.'

The Charmer

No woman can resist this chap's charms – or so he thinks. A dazzling smile, a compliment for every occasion and plenty of eye contact are his three major weapons and he's not afraid to use them. He won't be happy until he's won over every woman in the room, and he can't pass a glass-walled office or shop window without admiring his own reflection.

Most likely to say: 'My word, have you been working out?'

Will never say: 'Yes, your bum does look big in that.'

The Big Kid

He never really grew up and looks on his wife not only as his lover but also his mother and teacher. Refusing to take responsibility, he's unreliable, selfish and infuriating. He would rather be playing computer games than dealing with bills or tidying the house. Why would he want to face the trials of real life when he can live in his own childish fantasy world?

Most likely to say: 'Get out the way, it's Level twenty-seven!!'

Will never say: 'I really think we should talk about our investment portfolio.'

The Mummy's Boy

'I suppose when they reach a certain age some men are afraid to grow up. It seems the older the men get, the younger their new wives get.'
Elizabeth Taylor

He may not admit it, he may in some cases not even realize it, but mother will always be the main woman in this man's life. Nobody can cook like her and her rules on child-rearing are the ones that his wife should abide by. When life gets too much for him, he will run home to spend some time with his dear old mum, who will assure him that everything is okay and send him back on his way.

Most likely to say:	'That's not the way Mum used to do it.'
Will never say:	'Actually, I think my mother was totally wrong about that.'

The Textbook Husband

Although this man may well display certain elements of all of the above from time to time, for the most part he manages to keep them in check. The textbook husband is polite, courteous, attentive, affectionate, generous, well-spoken, mild-mannered and blessed with a marvellous sense of humour that never veers off into cheap smut or innuendo. Why, this chap ticks all the right boxes and can be held up as the model for all husbands! You may not be able to tick quite as many boxes as him, but if you tick the majority you'll be on the right lines.

Most likely to say: 'Really, it was nothing.'
Will never say: 'So what's in it for me?'

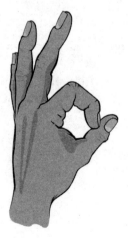

Jokes About Husbands

✳

A married man and his secretary are having an affair. After one passionate afternoon together he asks his secretary to take his shoes and rub them in some grass. She thinks it weird, but does as he asks.

When the man gets home, his wife asks him where he's been. He replies, 'I can't tell a lie. My secretary and I are having an affair. We left work early today, went to her place, made love all afternoon, and then fell asleep. That's why I'm late.'

His wife looks at him, notices his grass-stained shoes and says, 'You've been playing golf again, haven't you?'

'It first occurred to me that our marriage might be in trouble when my wife won an all expenses paid trip for two to Hawaii – and she went twice.'
Anonymous

✳

During the wedding rehearsal, the groom approached the vicar with an unusual offer.

'I'll give you £100 if you'll change the wedding vows so that when you get to the part where I'm to promise to 'love, honour and obey,' and 'forsaking all others, be faithful to her forever,' I'd appreciate it if you could just leave that part out,' he said. And he gave the vicar the money.

On the day of the wedding the vicar comes to the vows and says to the groom, 'Will you promise to prostrate yourself before her, obey her every command and wish, serve her breakfast in bed every morning of your life and swear eternally before God and your lovely wife that you will not even look at another woman, as long as you both shall live?'

The groom gulps, looks around and says in a small voice, 'I do.' Later, he says to the vicar, 'I thought we had a deal.'

The vicar gives him back his £100 and replies, 'She made me a much better offer.'

> *'An archaeologist is the best husband a woman can have. The older she gets the more interested he is in her.'*
> **Agatha Christie**

✷

Upon his engagement, a young man went to his father and said, 'Dad! I've found a woman just like mother.' His father replied, 'So what do you want? Sympathy?'

A man who had been married for sixty years was asked by a new groom the secret to a long and happy marriage, 'It's simple,' he replied. 'The man makes all the big decisions and the woman just makes the little decisions.'

'Does that really work?' said the young man. 'Oh yes,' he replied. 'Sixty years so far, and not one big decision.'

❋

The musician Eugen d'Albert was at a soiree when he introduced his new wife to an acquaintance, who replied 'Congratulations! You have rarely introduced me to so charming a wife.' Albert was married six times before he died.

❋

Lauren Bacall had a whimsical way of keeping husband Humphrey Bogart's ashes close. She has them put into an urn with a tiny gold whistle, which she had inscribed with the words, 'If you need anything, just whistle.' They formed the famous line from their favourite film together: *To Have and to Have Not.*

❋

Someone once asked General Mark Wayne Clark what was the best advice he had ever been given. 'To marry the girl I did,' he said. 'And who gave you that advice?' they asked. 'She did!'

❋

The French writer Honoré de Balzac once received a mysterious letter signed 'The Stranger'. He began a long affair with the writer, Evelina Hanska, who was then married to a Ukranian baron. The baron died in 1841, but Balzac didn't marry Evelina until five months before his own death in 1850. His reasons? 'It is easier to be a lover than a husband, for the same reason that it is more difficult to show a ready wit all day long than to produce an occasional bon mot.'

✳

American inventor Thomas Edison, who became deaf at a young age due to a bout of scarlet fever, suggested that his girlfriend learn Morse code in order to communicate with him. Some time later, he proposed to her – by tapping out a message on the palm of her hand. She answered yes, in Morse code, of course.

✳

After an argument, a husband said to his wife, 'You know, I was a fool when I married you'. She replied, 'Yes, dearest, but I was in love and didn't notice'.

✳

Once there were three men, Dave, John, and Mike, who were involved in a tragic car accident in which all three died. As they stood at the gates of heaven St Peter came up to them and said, 'You will all be given a method of transportation for your eternal use around heaven. You will be judged on your past deeds, and will have your transport chosen accordingly'.
St Peter looked at Dave and said, 'You, Dave, were a bad man. You cheated on your wife four times! For this, you will drive around heaven in a beaten up Transit van'.

Next St Peter looked at John and said, 'You, John, were not so bad, but you still cheated on your wife twice. For this, you will forever travel around heaven in a Volkwagon estate'.

St Peter finally looked at Sam, and said, 'You, Sam, are a shining example. You did not have sex until you were married, and you never cheated on your wife. For this, you shall be rewarded with a Ferrari'.

A short time later, Jon and Dave pulled up in their cars next to Sam's Ferrari and saw him sitting on the bonnet, his head in hands, sobbing. 'What's wrong, Sam?' they asked. 'You get to drive a Ferrari! Why are you so upset?'

Sam looked up and cried, 'I just saw my wife go by on a skate board!'

※

Jack often stopped at his favourite pub after a hard day's work to relax. He noticed a man next to him order a shot of vodka and a beer. The man drank the shot, chased it down with the beer and then looked into his shirt pocket.

This continued several times before Jack's curiosity got the better of him. He leaned over to the guy and said, 'Excuse me, I couldn't help but notice that little ritual. Why on earth do you look into your shirt pocket every time you drink your shot and pint?'

The man replied, 'There's a picture of my wife in there, and when she starts looking good, I'm heading home!'

※

A wife was reading the paper while her husband was watching the football. Suddenly, she burst out laughing. 'Listen to this,' she said. 'There's a classified ad here where a guy is offering to swap his wife for a season ticket to the stadium.'

'Hmmm,' her husband said, not taking his eyes off the screen. Teasing him, the wife said, 'Would you swap me for a season ticket?'

'Absolutely not,' he said. '

'How sweet,' the wife said. 'Why not?'

'Season's more than half over.'

Final Word

So now, the end is near – as you'll see from the fact it says The End at the bottom of this page. You have learned very well, wise husband, and reading *The Husband's Book* has elevated you to a higher level of marital awareness. For that you should be applauded, but one final word of warning before you go: do not fall into the trap of believing you are now the finished article. Where husbands are concerned, there is no such thing. You are without doubt a far more advanced husband than when you began reading this book, but you should always strive to improve. For starters, think about helping your wife with her coat every once in a while, or pulling the chair out for her when she sits down for dinner, or laying your coat across a big puddle like they used to do in old films. Or something.

The End.

Also available in this bestselling series:

The Wives' Book:
For The Wife Who's Best At Everything
ISBN 978-1-84317-352-0   Price: £9.99

The Boys' Book:
How To Be The Best At Everything
ISBN: 978-1-905158-64-5   Price: £7.99

The Girls' Book:
How To Be The Best At Everything
ISBN: 978-1-905158-79-9   Price: £7.99

The Mums' Book:
For The Mum Who's Best At Everything
ISBN: 978-1-84317-246-8   Price: £9.99

The Dads' Book:
For The Dad Who's Best At Everything
ISBN: 978-1-84317-250-5   Price: £9.99

The Grannies' Book:
For The Granny Who's Best At Everything
ISBN: 978-1-84317-251-2   Price: £9.99

The Grandads' Book:
For The Grandad Who's Best At Everything
ISBN 978-1-84317-308-3   Price: £9.99